Doping

Other Books of Related Interest

Opposing Viewpoints Series

Addiction

Behavioral Disorders

Dietary Supplements

Medical Testing

Prescription Drug Abuse

Professional Athletes

At Issue Series

Are Athletes Good Role Models?

Are Players' Unions Good for Professional Sports Leagues?

Club Drugs

Mexic's Drug War

Current Controversies Series

Prescription Drugs

Vaccines

"Congress shall make no law . . . abridging the freedom of speech, or of the press."

First Amendment to the US Constitution

The basic foundation of our democracy is the First Amendment guarantee of freedom of expression. The Opposing Viewpoints Series is dedicated to the concept of this basic freedom and the idea that it is more important to practice it than to enshrine it.

OPPOSING
VIEWPOINTS®
SERIES

I Doping

Margaret Haerens, Book Editor

GREENHAVEN PRESS
A part of Gale, Cengage Learning

GALE
CENGAGE Learning·

Farmington Hills, Mich • San Francisco • New York • Waterville, Maine
Meriden, Conn • Mason, Ohio • Chicago

Elizabeth Des Chenes, *Director, Content Strategy*
Cynthia Sanner, *Publisher*
Douglas Dentino, Manager, *New Product*

© 2014 Greenhaven Press, a part of Gale, Cengage Learning.

WCN: 01-100-101

Articles in Greenhaven Press anthologies are often edited for length to meet page require-ments. In addition, original titles of these works are changed to clearly present the main thesis and to explicitly indicate the author's opinion. Every effort is made to ensure that Greenhaven Press accurately reflects the original intent of the authors. Every effort has been made to trace the owners of copyrighted material.

Cover image © Dmitry Fisher/Shutterstock.com.

LIBRARY OF CONGRESS CATALOGING-IN-PUBLICATION DATA

Doping (Greenhaven Press)
   Doping / Margaret Haerens, book editor.
      pages cm. -- (Opposing viewpoints)
   Includes bibliographical references and index.
      ISBN 978-0-7377-6318-8 (hardcover) -- ISBN 978-0-7377-6319-5 (pbk.)
   1. Doping in sports--Moral and ethical aspects. I. Haerens, Margaret, editor of
compilation. II. Title.
   RC1230.D6575 2014
   617.1'027--dc23
                                                                    2013049846

Printed in the United States of America
1 2 3 4 5 6 7 18 17 16 15 14

Contents

Chapter 3: What Are the Effects of Doping on Sports?

Chapter 4: How Should Doping Athletes Be Treated?

Why Consider Opposing Viewpoints?

"The only way in which a human being can make some approach to knowing the whole of a subject is by hearing what can be said about it by persons of every variety of opinion and studying all modes in which it can be looked at by every character of mind. No wise man ever acquired his wisdom in any mode but this."

John Stuart Mill

In our media-intensive culture it is not difficult to find differing opinions. Thousands of newspapers and magazines and dozens of radio and television talk shows resound with differing points of view. The difficulty lies in deciding which opinion to agree with and which "experts" seem the most credible. The more inundated we become with differing opinions and claims, the more essential it is to hone critical reading and thinking skills to evaluate these ideas. Opposing Viewpoints books address this problem directly by presenting stimulating debates that can be used to enhance and teach these skills. The varied opinions contained in each book examine many different aspects of a single issue. While examining these conveniently edited opposing views, readers can develop critical thinking skills such as the ability to compare and contrast authors' credibility, facts, argumentation styles, use of persuasive techniques, and other stylistic tools. In short, the Opposing Viewpoints Series is an ideal way to attain the higher-level thinking and reading skills so essential in a culture of diverse and contradictory opinions.

In addition to providing a tool for critical thinking, Opposing Viewpoints books challenge readers to question their own strongly held opinions and assumptions. Most people form their opinions on the basis of upbringing, peer pressure, and personal, cultural, or professional bias. By reading carefully balanced opposing views, readers must directly confront new ideas as well as the opinions of those with whom they disagree. This is not to argue simplistically that everyone who reads opposing views will—or should—change his or her opinion. Instead, the series enhances readers' understanding of their own views by encouraging confrontation with opposing ideas. Careful examination of others' views can lead to the readers' understanding of the logical inconsistencies in their own opinions, perspective on why they hold an opinion, and the consideration of the possibility that their opinion requires further evaluation.

Evaluating Other Opinions

To ensure that this type of examination occurs, Opposing Viewpoints books present all types of opinions. Prominent spokespeople on different sides of each issue as well as well-known professionals from many disciplines challenge the reader. An additional goal of the series is to provide a forum for other, less known, or even unpopular viewpoints. The opinion of an ordinary person who has had to make the decision to cut off life support from a terminally ill relative, for example, may be just as valuable and provide just as much insight as a medical ethicist's professional opinion. The editors have two additional purposes in including these less known views. One, the editors encourage readers to respect others' opinions—even when not enhanced by professional credibility. It is only by reading or listening to and objectively evaluating others' ideas that one can determine whether they are worthy of consideration. Two, the inclusion of such viewpoints encourages the important critical thinking skill of objectively evaluating an author's credentials and bias. This evaluation will illuminate an author's reasons for taking a particular stance on an issue and will aid in readers' evaluation of the author's ideas.

It is our hope that these books will give readers a deeper understanding of the issues debated and an appreciation of the complexity of even seemingly simple issues when good and honest people disagree. This awareness is particularly important in a democratic society such as ours in which people enter into public debate to determine the common good. Those with whom one disagrees should not be regarded as enemies but rather as people whose views deserve careful examination and may shed light on one's own.

Thomas Jefferson once said that "difference of opinion leads to inquiry, and inquiry to truth." Jefferson, a broadly educated man, argued that "if a nation expects to be ignorant and free . . . it expects what never was and never will be." As individuals and as a nation, it is imperative that we consider the opinions of others and examine them with skill and discernment. The Opposing Viewpoints Series is intended to help readers achieve this goal.

David L. Bender and Bruno Leone,
Founders

Introduction

"We all should know by now that the fight against doping in sport has reached the stage where science alone will not eradicate cheating or very often even detect it."

—David Howard,
director general of the
World Anti-Doping Agency

Doping is the practice of taking drugs or other substances to improve physical performance. It can be traced back to ancient Greece, where athletes who participated in the first Olympic Games ingested extracts of mushrooms, plant seeds, and herbal stimulants to give them enhanced strength and endurance. During the time of the Roman Empire, gladiators used caffeine, strychnine (a poison that when taken in small doses, stimulates the nervous system), herbal potions, and special foods to give them more energy and focus for their fights in coliseums. Chariot racers doped their horses to win races. Across different cultures and eras, athletes have turned to various herbs, drugs, and diets to improve physical performance and get the edge in athletic competitions.

The word *doping* first appeared in an English dictionary in 1879. It is thought to derive from the Dutch word *dop*, which is the name of an alcoholic beverage used by Zulu warriors to provide energy during battle and ceremonial dances. In the West *doping* came to mean the use of performance-enhancing drugs (PEDs) in sports.

In 1886 an English cyclist became the first athlete to die from PEDs. Arthur Linton died from an overdose of trimethyl, which is used for increased strength and endurance, during a race in France. In 1904 American Thomas Hicks injected strychnine and drank brandy during the marathon at the Olympic Games in the United States. He won the race but collapsed after his victory and almost died.

By the 1920s doping was recognized as a considerable problem in sports. International sporting federations began to take steps to address it. In 1928 the International Association of Athletics Federations banned the use of any substance that could stimulate physical performance, but because there was no testing for banned substances, athletes continued to use them, developing ways to evade detection by authorities. Doping bans were adopted by many other international sporting federations by the mid–twentieth century. In 1963 France became the first country to enact antidoping legislation. Other countries soon followed.

The development of amphetamines and synthetic hormones during the 1930s led to a new era in doping. Athletes began to rely on amphetamines for added energy and on synthetic hormones to build muscle and endurance. At the 1952 Olympic Games in Finland, doping was endemic. Syringes and vials were found lying around in changing rooms. Several speed skaters fell ill after injecting amphetamines right before competitions.

There were also high-profile deaths during this period from amphetamine doping. In 1960 at the Olympics in Italy, Danish cyclist Knud Enemark Jensen died during the 100m team time trials. It was later determined that Jensen had traces of several banned substances in his blood, including amphetamine. At the 1967 Tour de France, a famous cycling race held annually in France and neighboring countries, British cyclist Tommy Simpson died of an amphetamine overdose.

In 1966 both professional cycling and soccer instituted the first systematic PED testing of athletes at world championship competitions. In 1967 the International Olympic Committee (IOC), the governing body for the Olympic Games, put together its first prohibited substances list and instituted a medical committee to oversee an antidoping program. The IOC implemented its first system of drug testing at the 1968 Olympics in Mexico.

As drug testing of athletes became more widespread, cheating trainers, managers, doctors, and athletes began turning to new drugs, such as anabolic steroids, to avoid detection. During the 1970s, anabolic steroids were used widely in weightlifting and other strength sports. At the 1976 Olympics in Canada observers suspected that the East German women's swim team was doping when they won eleven out of thirteen events. Many years later, German authorities proved that the team's coaches had injected the athletes with anabolic steroids without their knowledge or consent. At the 1988 Olympics in Korea world-renowned Canadian sprinter Ben Johnson tested positive for anabolic steroids.

The emergence of erythropoietin (EPO), a synthetic hormone that increases the flow of oxygen to the muscles, in the late 1980s was a boon to cyclists willing to risk their life and career for athletic glory. One of the biggest EPO scandals in sports was the Festina affair, during the 1998 Tour de France. It began with the arrest of a Festina team member who had PEDs in his possession and that lead to a massive investigation. Festina eventually admitted that the team was engaged in systematic doping, and race officials expelled the entire team from the Tour de France. The revelations that there was systematic doping at the biggest cycling competition in the world affirmed the suspicions of fans that EPO was a pervasive problem at the highest levels of professional cycling.

In 1999 international efforts to combat doping in sports took a huge step with the founding of the World Anti-Doping Agency (WADA), which was created to set standards for antidoping programs and coordinate antidoping efforts among athletes, government agencies, international sporting federations, and international agencies. Despite the advancement in testing, the enhanced cooperation and coordination, the increased publicity for antidoping efforts, and the harsh sanctions imposed on doping athletes, the problem continued into the twenty-first century.

Today WADA uses investigative work to prove that athletes are doping. It builds cases against cheating athletes through a combination of drug testing, eyewitness testimony, medical and financial records, and other documentation. Law enforcement, immigration authorities, and custom officials have all become valuable partners with WADA to enforce doping bans and uncover systematic cheating.

In American sports one of the biggest doping scandals is the steroid era in professional baseball, which lasted from the late 1980s through the late 2000s. Although Major League Baseball, the governing organization for the sport, had instituted a doping ban in 1991, widespread testing did not begin until 2003. For more than a decade, PEDs flourished, with many of baseball's premier players, such as Barry Bonds, Mark McGwire, Sammy Sosa, and Roger Clemens, suspected of using steroids.

In October 2007 American sprinter Marion Jones admitted that she had used PEDs for years, including EPO, and had lied to federal authorities about it. She was sentenced to six months in prison and two years probation and community service for the perjury and for check fraud unrelated to the perjury. The IOC stripped her of the five gold medals she won at the 2000 Olympics in Australia, and she was also forced to give back all other prizes she had earned in competition since 2000.

One of the biggest doping scandals in sports exploded in June 2012, when the United States Anti-Doping Agency (USADA) charged American champion cyclist Lance Armstrong with doping and drug trafficking. Allegations had been made against Armstrong and his US Postal cycling team for years regarding the use of EPO and human growth hormone. A lengthy investigation, including two positive drug tests and the testimony of several ex-teammates and associates, led to the USADA charges and a lifetime ban from cycling. Initially Armstrong denied the charges and vowed to clear his name. In January 2013, however, Armstrong finally admitted to using PEDs during his athletic career, and Tour de France officials stripped him of his record seven wins. The USADA's report concludes that Armstrong engaged in "the most sophisticated, professionalized and successful doping program that sport has ever seen."

Fighting doping in sports is a challenge for antidoping authorities, who are constantly confronted by new drugs and new technology. This book explores these challenges and possible solutions in the following chapters: Why Do Athletes Dope?, Should Doping Be Banned?, What Are the Effects of Doping on Sports?, and How Should Doping Athletes Be Treated? The information in this book provides insight into recent controversies regarding the efficacy of doping bans in sports and the treatment of doping athletes. This book also explores the impact of doping on an athlete's body, on the level of competition, and on the integrity of sports.

OPPOSING
VIEWPOINTS®
SERIES

I Why Do Athletes Dope?

Chapter Preface

Throughout history some athletes have chosen to use drugs or other substances that improved their athletic performance, allowing them to push their physical limits during competition. Technological advances by the pharmaceutical industry have resulted in performance-enhancing drugs (PEDs) that are hard to detect. For athletic officials, sports organizations and committees, and professional sports leagues, developing new testing procedures to detect doping has been a formidable challenge.

Erythropoietin (EPO) is a prime example of this challenge. Produced naturally by the human body, EPO is a hormone that stimulates red blood cell production, which in turn increases the amount of oxygen that the blood can carry to the body's muscles. For athletes, this means increased endurance during athletic performance. However, there are dangerous side effects in taking EPO. Because EPO thickens the blood, use of the drug can cause stroke, heart disease, and fatal heart attack.

Once pharmaceutical companies were able to produce a synthetic EPO in the late 1980s, however, athletes and trainers quickly determined that using the synthetic EPO was worth the health risks to significantly improve athletic endurance—especially at the end of a competition, when some extra energy can make the difference between winning and losing.

By 1990, synthetic EPO use was common in cycling. Although it was banned by the World Anti-Doping Agency (WADA) in the early 1990s, a large number of elite riders continued to use the drug in training and competition. It was even blamed for the death of a number of cyclists, including World Champion and Olympic medalist Joachim Halupczok of Poland.

In May 2007 several former riders for Telekom, a German cycling team, revealed that they had used EPO on several occasions during the 1990s, a decade in which they had become one of the dominant powers in international cycling. One of Telekom's most successful riders, Bjarne Riis of Denmark, won the 1996 Tour de France, a famous cycling race that takes place every year in France and neighboring countries. Riis later admitted that he had been doping and race officials subsequently wiped him from the record books.

During the 1998 Tour de France, an investigation revealed widespread doping among elite cycling teams. French authorities detained and arrested team members, several cyclists dropped out of the race, and eventually race officials expelled the entire Festina team from the race. Known as the Festina affair, the scandal reaffirmed the suspicions of fans around the world that EPO was a pervasive problem at the highest levels of professional cycling. The revelations of EPO abuse that emerged after multiple investigations, especially in the case of American cyclist Lance Armstrong, would severely damage the sport.

At the 2000 Olympics in Sydney, Australia, an effective and reliable test for synthetic EPO was finally introduced. However, doping cyclists were already turning to new forms of EPO, many of which could not be detected by the new test. As medical science develops and releases new PEDs, there will always be athletes willing to take them in order to get a competitive advantage—no matter the risk to career or health. The challenge for WADA is to stay on top of doping trends and quickly develop tests to catch doping athletes.

The threat posed by new drugs and technology to Olympic and professional sports is one of the subjects examined in the following chapter, which explores why athletes dope. Viewpoints focus on the benefits and risks of doping, as well as factors that encourage athletes to consider taking PEDs.

> *"Libertarians of the sport world who say athletes should be free to do what they want to their bodies neglect an aspect of PEDs' [performance-enhancing drugs] health risks: The effect on young athletes when doping pervades a sport."*

Doping Can Harm Athletes

Scott Douglas

In the following viewpoint, Scott Douglas contends that performance-enhancing drugs (PEDs) pose a danger to athletes' health. He identifies the most popular types of PEDs and the health risks that they pose, concluding that PEDs are banned not only because their use is unethical, but also because they can kill. Scott Douglas is a journalist and a news editor for Runner's World *magazine.*

As you read, consider the following questions:

1. According to Scott Douglas, when was the World Anti-Doping Agency established?

2. When was blood doping banned, according to Douglas?

3. According to Douglas, when was gene doping banned?

As in most discussions of the topic, Lance Armstrong's everyone-was-doing-it rationale for using performance-enhancing drugs focused on ethics and availability. This emphasis ignores a fundamental reason why PEDs are banned—they can kill you.

The World Anti-Doping Agency (WADA) was created in 1999 to systematize and enforce a long list of prohibited performance-enhancing drugs and practices. (The U.S. Anti-Doping Agency, which Armstrong fought for so long, is the American branch of WADA.) WADA generally prohibits something if it meets at least two of three criteria:

- it improves athletic performance

- it violates what WADA calls "the spirit of sport"

- it poses a health risk to athletes

The need to protect elite athletes from themselves is real. In surveys administered between 1982 and 1995, half of elite athletes said they would take an undetectable PED if doing so meant they would win an Olympic gold medal, even if the drug were guaranteed to kill them within five years. When that hypothetical was posed to 250 normal Australians, less than one percent said they would take the gold-then-death drug.

The Effect on Young Athletes

Libertarians of the sport world who say athletes should be free to do what they want to their bodies neglect an aspect of PEDs' health risks: The effect on young athletes when doping pervades a sport. Alex Hutchinson, who ran for Canada in the world cross country championships and writes a column about science and fitness for [the newspaper] *The Globe and Mail*, puts it this way: "If you allow doping, then there's a trickle-down effect. You'll have to dope just to get to the professional level, at which point you'll have doctors supervising your red blood cell count and so on. So it's the kids who will be most at risk, forced to dope just to reach the level where doping can be done 'safely.'"

Note that cost doesn't factor into this attempt to create a level playing field. The blood booster EPO [erythropoietin], one of Armstrong's go-tos, is prohibited, but hyperbaric chambers, which simulate high altitude and therefore theoretically impart some of the benefits of EPO, aren't. Three-time American Olympic runner Dathan Ritzenhein spends 12–14 hours a day in his sealed-off bedroom; the device that simulates high altitude in the room costs between $15,000 and $20,000, depending on the size of the room. A month's supply of EPO for a cheating endurance athlete can cost just a few hundred dollars.

There are some oddities on the list of banned substances, if we're considering the combination of athletic boost and health risk. Marijuana and heroin (!) are prohibited, although it's hard to imagine a scenario where you would say, "I would have won if the guy who beat me wasn't strung out." Caffeine, meanwhile, was removed from the banned list in 2004, even though it's a proven performance enhancer that, when taken in excess, can land you in the hospital. . . .

Blood Boosters

Blood boosters are used primarily by endurance athletes to increase the oxygen-carrying capacity of their blood. EPO, a drug used to treat anemia in cancer patients getting chemotherapy, is the best known, and not just because of the irony of Armstrong's post-cancer embrace of it [Armstrong was treated for testicular cancer in 1996]. Early attempts to cheat with EPO were often fatal. In the late 1980s and early 1990s, at least 20 elite European cyclists died suddenly while sleeping or at rest, as did seven Swedish orienteerers [cross-country racers]. The deaths are now attributed to EPO, which increases hematocrit, or the percentage of red blood cells in blood. Too much EPO causes the phenomenon known as "blood to mud": as hematocrit gets higher, blood gets thicker. The risk of blood clots, which can lead to stroke or heart attack, increases. "Thick blood" is even more dangerous when athletes get dehydrated, as tends to happen when you ride or run hard for hours at a time.

A urine test for EPO was introduced in 2001, by which time dopers better knew how to use EPO without killing themselves. When the EPO test came out, some athletes reverted to a more old-school version of blood boosting known as blood doping, in which the athlete receives a blood transfusion (either someone else's or their own). This is what Armstrong's former teammate Tyler Hamilton admitted to, which cost him the gold medal he had won at the 2004 Olympics. Blood doping carries not only the blood-to-mud risk of EPO but also the small but significant contamination risk inherent in any blood transfusion. Blood doping wasn't prohibited until 1986.

Anabolic Steroids

Anabolic steroids are most often used by athletes in power sports to build muscle and shorten recovery time. The list of health risks is long, as is the list of elite athletes who are known to or widely suspected of using them: Jose Canseco, Roger Clemens, and Barry Bonds in baseball; Bill Romanowski and Shawne Merriman in football; and Marion Jones, Ben Johnson, and basically every Eastern European Olympian of the 1970s in track and field. Oh, and of course cycling— testosterone is considered an anabolic steroid, and is what Floyd Landis got busted for.

You know a PED is prevalent when it gets its own phrase. "Roid rage," or uncontrollable aggression, stems from taking anabolic steroids. So do kidney and liver damage, plus shrunken testicles and enlarged breasts in men and facial hair, a deepened voice, and enlarged clitoris in women. Writing last year in [the journal] *Forensic Science International*, Italian doc-

What Is Gene Therapy?

Gene therapy has a number of different definitions, but in essence, it is the manipulation of expression of specific genes in the body of the patient. This may be achieved by delivery of a functional version of the gene that is defective and this is the most common approach to single-gene disorders, such as haemophilia A and B, cystic fibrosis and DMD [Duchenne muscular dystrophy]. Alternatively, gene transfer can be used to deliver genes encoding proteins that modify an acquired disease, such as infection or ischaemic heart disease. Finally, gene transfer can be used to downregulate gene expression to avoid the activity of a harmful gene or to modify a response to a specific stimulus. A particular advantage of gene therapy compared to other treatments, such as the administration of recombinant proteins, is that by continuous production of the protein *in vivo*, one avoids the peak and trough pharmacodynamics associated with a series of injections.

D.J. Wells, "Gene Doping: The Hype and the Reality,"
British Journal of Pharmacology, June 2008.

tors described four cases (three bodybuilders, one cyclist) of fatal cardiac failure in steroid users.

Human Growth Hormone

Human growth hormone [(HGH)] is often used by the same sorts of athletes who get performance boosts from steroids; Marion Jones isn't the only busted Olympian to have taken it in conjunction with steroids. Armstrong also took HGH. It can lead to heart failure, arthritis and its outward tell-tale sign: acromegaly, or disfigurement of the jaw, skull, hands and feet. Track and field fans tend to get suspicious when sprinters in their twenties suddenly get braces at the same time their performances improve.

Dopers are almost always ahead of the testers. The next great area of exploration for athletic cheaters is likely to be gene doping, or genetically modifying muscle cells.

Gene Doping

Gene doping has been banned since 2003, even though there's no evidence anyone is doing it. But if and when it becomes common, look out, because it could be like cheating on, well, steroids—potentially greater performance effects with less detectability. The potential health risks read like they're ripped from a science fiction movie, including immune reactions gone haywire, overexpression of the desired genetic trait, and gene silencing, or "turning off" the gene one is trying to manipulate.

And while such a scenario remains theoretical at this point, it's possible that gene doping could be practiced via germline gene therapy methods, which target sperm or egg cells. This could result in genetic modifications being passed to future generations, in which case the sins of the cheating father will be visited upon the son.

| *"It's not that steroids are perfectly safe.*
But why single them out?"

Steroids Hysteria

John Stossel

In the following viewpoint, written in May 2009, John Stossel interviews a doctor who contends that steroids "do horrible things" to people and that they should be banned. Stossel also speaks with a bioethicist who maintains that much of the infor-mation about the dangers of performance-enhancing drugs (PEDs), particularly steroids, is hype and hysteria. Stossel con-cludes that there is not much evidence that steroids are risky and that adults should have the right to do whatever they want with their own bodies. John Stossel is a journalist, an author, and the host of the television show Stossel *on the Fox Business Network.*

As you read, consider the following questions:

1. According to John Stossel, who is the doctor that testi-fied to Congress that steroids do horrible things?

2. According to Stossel, what side effects are associated with steroid use?

3. Besides steroids, what other risky drug was Tayler Hooton taking at the time of his death, according to Stossel?

With the return of baseball and a new book on Alex Rodriguez released this week, a fresh round of congressional posturing about steroids is upon us.

Why is it Congress's business?

I asked U.S. Reps. Elijah Cummings, D-Md., and Cliff Stearns, R-Fla., about that for my next TV special, "Don't Even Think about Saying That!," which will air this Friday on ABC.

"This is part of our duty," Cummings says, "to protect the American people." Steroids are "a serious public-health problem."

Stearns added, "Teenagers commit suicide."

And Congress will fix it all.

Of course, people like Dr. Gary Wadler testify in Congress that steroids do horrible things.

"The threat is dying! The threat is suicide!" Wadler told me.

I'd heard such scary claims for years. Death by steroids. "Roid rage" worthy of after-school specials.

Years ago, when a pro wrestler beat me up, I was told that steroids drove him to do it. Steroids were blamed for wrestler Chris Benoit killing himself and his family, and teenage baseball star Taylor Hooton's suicide.

But Dr. Norman Fost, a bioethicist at the University of Wisconsin, says it's all bunk. The anti-steroid movement, he says, is filled with hysteria and hype.

"The horror stories about the medical claims . . . some of them are just frankly made up."

Fost insists there's no correlation between injectable steroids and brain tumors.

To my surprise, Wadler admits that's true. And he's not so certain about other claims. When I asked him if steroids cause strokes, he said, "It's on a possible list."

Heart attack?

"The likelihood of anabolic steroid abuse being associated with heart disease is real."

Note the waffle words like "possible" and "associated." He uses them because—unlike smoking and cancer—there are *no* long-term epidemiological studies that show steroids *cause* those diseases.

Every drug is "associated" with side effects. Advil is associated with ulcers and shock.

It's not that steroids are perfectly safe. But why single them out?

"We don't stop Natasha Richardson from skiing," Fost notes.

"We don't stop people from eating lemon meringue pie . . . People everywhere take enormous risks way greater than even the hyped-up risks of steroids."

Yes, steroids use is associated with hair loss, acne, testicular atrophy and even growing male breasts. But Fost says those side effects would be minimized if steroids were legal.

"If athletes are going to use these things, it would be better to have them on the table where informed doctors can help them get the right drug with the right dose and fewer side effects.

That's not good enough for Wadler. "I don't think you supervise . . . the abuse of a drug."

For Wadler, "abuse" is any use that's not medically necessary. But entire fields of medicine are devoted to "unnecessary" procedures—breast enhancement, hair replacement, etc. Consenting adults should be free to do pretty much whatever they like to their own bodies.

If steroids are such a terrible threat, there must be lots of high-profile deaths. But Wadler couldn't cite any.

The Chris Benoit 'roid-rage murders and suicide? The medical examiner later said there was no evidence proving the testosterone he was taking caused the crimes. There's evidence that steroids can increase aggression in some people, but, Fost says, "The overwhelming examples of criminal behavior by professional athletes has nothing to do with steroids."

Taylor Hooton's suicide?

"There's no evidence of steroids producing suicidal behavior."

Hooton was taking *other* risky drugs like Lexapro, which has been shown to cause suicidal thinking.

That wrestler who hit me later said he did it because his boss told him to.

Health issues aside, what about sportsmanship?

"I don't know why you would think this is cheating any more than the hundred of other things athletes do to enhance their performance," Fost said.

Tiger Woods improved his eyesight with surgery. "Janet Evans won a gold medal in swimming," Fost noted, "and bragged about a greasy swimsuit that she was sure had a lot to do with her victory."

Wadler defends the anti-steroid rule because "abuse represents a significant risk to health and, in fact, enhances a criminal element."

But there's only a criminal element because zealots like Wadler insist on making steroid use illegal!

"If doping starts to make you question greatness when you see it, they are losing a fan."

Doping Undermines the Integrity of Competition

Tim Burns

In the following viewpoint, Tim Burns maintains that doping reduces athletic competition to a scientific competition. In essence, the competition is really a scientific experiment that determines which doping regime is more effective on any given day. Burns also argues that doping tarnishes cherished sports memories and disillusions loyal fans. He concludes that the use of performance-enhancing drugs (PEDs) is still rife in professional sports because it works. Tim Burns is a contributor to The Yarn *website.*

As you read, consider the following questions:

1. According to Tim Burns, what English cyclist collapsed and died while racing in the Tour de France in 1967?

2. How many Tour de France winners since 1998 were not subsequently banned for doping during their career, according to Tim Burns?

3. Which cyclist in the 2013 Tour de France did Burns suspect of doping?

[Swiss tennis player] Martina Hingis, [Australian cricketer] Shane Warne, [American cyclist] Lance Armstrong, [Australian rules footballer] Jobe Watson, [American baseball player] Barry Bonds, [American basketball player] O.J. Mayo and [American football player] Shawne Merriman. All of these individuals have been accused of taking a banned substance while in competition since the turn of the [twenty-first] century. The sports are as diverse as the substances ranging from the recreational (cocaine) through weight loss and masking agents (diuretics) to the full-measure blood doping (EPO [erythropoietin]) and steroids (such as DHEA). The cocaine trace that caused Hingis to suffer a two-year ban may have been due to a lack of awareness or a lapse in self control but the other substances provide a clear performance benefit and have corresponding penalties as decreed by the World Anti-Doping Agency (WADA). Despite the penalties, the crackdowns, the campaigns and the rhetoric, performance enhancing substance use in the sporting world is still rife. Why? And at what cost?

Doping Works

We will not find out the result of ASADA [Australian Sports Anti-Doping Authority] investigation into [biochemist] Steven Dank and Essendon [an Australian football club] until the 1st of August [2013] at the earliest. However WADA's reaction to Jobe Watson's admission provides some insight into the likely ramifications. WADA have indicated that they do not care how a banned substance got into a players system for the purpose of prosecution. If Jobe goes, the 2012 Brownlow Medal will become another honour to be rescinded on the basis of doping.

Doping has a fantastic winning record. The 100 metres sprint is the Blue Riband of the Summer Olympics and a race that earned the title of "the dirtiest race in history"—from less than 13 seconds in Seoul in 1988. This week [July 2013] it emerged that [American] Tyson Gay and [Jamaican] Asafa Powell have continued the tradition of sprinters besmirching the image of track athletics with both returning positive tests for banned substances. Gay's personal records as the fastest man in 2013 and the second fastest man of all time will likely be stricken from the record books. But these athletes are not "victims of doping"—they are the poster boys.

The Tour de France

Doping in July—it must be the Tour de France. No sport has failed so spectacularly to contain doping than cycling. Tommy Simpson was one of the greatest British riders of all time and following his collapse and death on the slopes of Mont Ventoux [France] in 1967 mandatory testing for all cyclists was introduced. A rumoured combination of amphetamines and alcohol (riders used brandy to dull the pain) lead to the death of the 29 year old, although no inquest was ever conducted. Doping has continued within cycling for decades spurred on by the success of its proponents.

The biggest advocates of performance enhancers are those who have publicly condemned it—look to [Belgian cyclist] Eddy Merckx of the 1970s, or more recently Lance Armstrong. Both widely condemned fellow riders while simultaneously enjoying the success and plaudits that flowed from doping. The rampant use has had a sad result on cycling's most famous event [the Tour de France] with only three winners since 1998 not subsequently being banned for doping during their career. Only one fifth of people on the top step of the [winner's] podium in Paris have remained free from doping. That is enough to hurt any sport.

So why do it? It is just math—with 12/15 wins—riders are 400% more likely to win with doping than without . . . the glory of that moment outweighs the fear of future repercussions.

Banned for Life

In June 2012, legendary bicyclist Lance Armstrong (1971–) faced multiple charges by the U.S. Anti-Doping Association (USADA). The USADA claimed to have previously unreleased evidence, including blood samples and testimony of witnesses, that Armstrong was consistently guilty of "blood manipulation" during his long career as a competitive cyclist while on the US Postal Service team. Armstrong firmly denied the charges. Armstrong won the grueling Tour de France a record seven times in a row (from 1999 through 2005) after surviving brain, lung, and testicular cancer. In late August 2012, he was stripped of his seven Tour de France titles and received a lifetime ban after deciding not to contest doping charges brought against him by the USADA. Armstrong failed to block charges in U.S. federal court, leading to his statement that he did not believe he could "confront the allegations in a fair setting." On 10 October, the USADA released a thousand page report with evidence showing that "beyond any doubt the US Postal Service Pro Cycling Team ran the most sophisticated, professionalized, and successful doping program the sport has ever seen." The report detailed evidence, including financial payments, laboratory test results, and sworn testimony from twenty-six people, including eleven of Armstrong's former teammates, of the highly refined doping conspiracy. Dr. Michele Ferrari and Dr. Garcia del Moral, two other members of the US Postal Service team, received lifetime bans for their involvement in the drug ring.

"Sports and Drug Use,"
Global Issues in Context Online Collection.
Detroit, MI: Gale, 2013.

The Cost

I recently read a thoughtful discussion that suggested that 100% accurate testing would ruin sport and that the decision-makers in sport encourage doping to produce the best spectacle. I disagree.

I watched Armstrong in 2003, 2004, and 2005 battle [Italian cyclist] Ivan Basso and [German cyclist] Jan Ullrich through the mountain stages, leaving the peloton [main group of racers] far behind. It was an epic battle. Unfortunately, looking back it was a farce, all three have been banned for doping and when the illusion falls away I realise I was watching competing EPO products and doping systems. In essence I was following competing scientific experiments. If doping starts to make you question greatness when you see it, they are losing a fan.

Pick your sport, pick your moment.

- [Australian rules footballer] Nick Davis in the last quarter of the semi-final against Geelong in 2005

- [Australian swimmer Ian] Thorpe bringing home the 4×100 freestyle team in Sydney [Olympic Games] in 2000

- [racehorse] Makybe Diva wins back-to-back-to-back Melbourne Cups in 2005

- [Australian football player John] Aloisi puts Australia into the FIFA World Cup Finals in 2005

Imagine having those moments tarnished. These are the moments that breed fans and without them sport will wither. Sports are funded by the fans, in the stadiums, in the merchandising and in the membership. Decision-makers want a spectacle, but fierce competition would still exist without doping and the risk to their livelihood is too great. . . .

Moments of Greatness

In the 2006 Tour de France, [American cyclist] Floyd Landis lost a huge amount of time on stage 16, gave up the yellow jersey and looked to be a spent force. The next day, as I watched on, Landis rode off the front of the peloton, decimating his rivals and recovering all but 30 seconds of the time he had lost the previous day. That was a moment, one man fighting to remain in contention dragging himself over the gruelling final climb alone—he was peerless that day. Landis won the Tour but was stripped of the title following a positive test from stage 17. That moment has gone.

I have not seen a moment comparable in the Tour, until this year [2013]. On Sunday night, I watched [Britain's] Chris Froome leave his team and a collective of the best cyclists on the planet seemingly stationary on the final climb of the day. The Sky Pro-cycling team is not as strong as the team that rode [Britain Bradley] Wiggins to victory last year and after [Australian] Richie Porte cracked Froome was left to climb alone. One kilometre from the summit of Mont Ventoux— approximately where fellow British rider Tommy Simpson collapsed almost 50 years earlier—Froome kicked past the last of his rivals and stormed home to a famous victory, further extending his yellow jersey lead.

It was a moment of greatness. Let's hope I can keep this one.

"The joke among riders of the era was that drug tests weren't actually drug tests—they were I.Q. tests, easily beaten through evasion and careful dosage, as well as the overarching fact that the medical sophistication of the testers lagged several years behind that of the athletes."

How Lance Armstrong Is Like Lehman Bros.

Daniel Coyle

In the following viewpoint, Daniel Coyle compares the doping scandal in professional cycling to the world of finance. He argues that both are characterized by a culture of excess and risk, a record of success and high performance, and then a catastrophic fall. Coyle explains that both professional cycling and the world of finance were enabled by a cheating culture, a lack of regulation, and a compliant and unquestioning media. American cyclist Lance Armstrong, who was at the center of the cycling scandal, excelled in cycling's doping culture because he had the most money, the best resources, and a personality that charmed cycling officials, reporters, and fans. Coyle suggests that Armstrong

Daniel Coyle, "How Lance Armstrong is Like Lehman Bros." *Slate*, October 17, 2012. Copyright © 2012 by Slate. All rights reserved. Reproduced by permission.

simply became "too big to fail." Daniel Coyle is a best-selling author. His books include Lance Armstrong's War, The Secret Race: Inside the Hidden World of the Tour de France *(cowritten with American cyclist Tyler Hamilton), and* The Talent Code.

As you read, consider the following questions:

1. According to Daniel Coyle, who was Lance Armstrong's greatest commercial supporter?

2. By how much does Coyle estimate that EPO improved endurance in professional cyclists?

3. How much did Armstrong spend on maintaining his exclusive relationship with Dr. Michele Ferrari, according to Coyle?

It keeps getting worse for Lance Armstrong. On Wednesday [October 17, 2012], a week after the U. S. Anti-Doping Agency released its devastating 1,000-page report on the cyclist's doping, the seven-time Tour de France winner stepped down as the chairman of his cancer charity, Livestrong. Armstrong's greatest commercial supporter, Nike, also announced it is severing ties with him. "Due to the seemingly insurmountable evidence that Lance Armstrong participated in doping and misled Nike for more than a decade, it is with great sadness that we have terminated our contract with him," the company explained in a statement.

Sports and Wall Street

The Armstrong story is a familiar one, and it leaves us in the frustrating position of asking why our top athletes keep choosing to dope, cover up, and end up disgraced. While it's tempting to explain Armstrong's fall through traditional notions of temptation and sin, it might be more useful to look to the world of finance and Wall Street. In both cases, a culture of excess and risk led to record-breaking performances, and then to catastrophe. In both cases, the behavior in question was driven by a distinct set of social forces, including a win-at-all-costs culture, lack of regulation, and the credulousness of journalists and the public.

In many ways, the structure of professional cycling resembles a trading floor: small, tightly knit teams competing daily, with great intensity and effort, for marginal rewards. A single percentage point can make the difference between winning and losing.

Just as Wall Street firms hired Ivy League PhDs [well-educated people with doctorate degrees] to invent new financial instruments, so did cycling teams hire doctors to perfect new pharmacological instruments. The mid-1990s brought the introduction of the blood-booster EPO [erythropoietin], which improved endurance by 10 to 20 percent, and which, perhaps more important, was undetectable. When professional riders began using EPO, their improvement was such that others were left with a simple choice. According to Armstrong's former teammate—and my co-author on the book *The Secret Race*—Tyler Hamilton, "For me, it was either start cheating along with them, or go home."

A few chose to go home. Those who stayed, like Hamilton, found themselves in a chemical arms race. Riders and doctors began pushing farther, augmenting EPO with insulin, human growth hormone, testosterone, artificial hemoglobin, and the medieval but highly effective method of banking and reinfusing one's own blood.

A Lack of Regulation

They did so largely without fear of being caught. During the Armstrong era, cyclists regarded drug testers with the same nod-and-wink aloofness with which Wall Street firms regarded the SEC [US Securities and Exchange Commission]. The joke among riders of the era was that drug tests weren't actually drug tests—they were I.Q. tests, easily beaten through evasion and careful dosage, as well as the overarching fact that the medical sophistication of the testers lagged several years behind that of the athletes. Spurred on by their fear of being outmaneuvered, teams and riders sought ever-more aggressive methods. During the 2000 Tour de France, Hamilton reinfused one pint of his own blood. By 2004, his regimen called for three pints.

Many of us instinctively presume that cheating creates a level playing field. In fact, it does precisely the reverse. Widespread cheating rewards the few who have the best information, the most money, and the highest risk tolerance. In this world, Armstrong and his team ruled: Armstrong spent more than $1 million maintaining his exclusive relationship with Dr. Michele Ferrari, regarded as the sport's best doping doctor. Armstrong used his private jet to transport drugs, and he cultivated a friendly working relationship with the sport's governing body that, according to the USADA report, may have helped him evade sanction for a suspicious drug test in 2001. Armstrong also had an entrepreneurial attitude toward risk, hiring his gardener to follow the 1999 Tour de France on a motorcycle and deliver EPO.

A Turning Point

While a few intrepid journalists were farsighted enough to cast doubt on the validity of Armstrong and Postal's [his team's] dominant performances, most were content to focus on the myth-like story they witnessed on the road each July. Only in 2010, when the federal government and USADA began their respective investigations, did the truth begin to emerge. Thanks to investigators and the riders who have stepped forward, cycling now faces its watershed moment: an opportunity to build a culture of meaningful regulation, accountability, and to ensure a clean sport for future generations.

The Armstrong era happened because doping worked so powerfully and lucratively that no one—not riders, not cycling's governing body, not the media—was willing to stop it. It was a time of hollow magic. It helped create kings and heroes that were too big to fail.

Until, all at once, they weren't.

| "A new substance that is hard to spot today might be easy to detect the day after tomorrow."

New Drugs and Technology Make It Easier to Dope and Evade Testing Procedures

Richard Williams

In the following viewpoint, written in May 2013, Richard Williams suggests that Italian cyclist Danilo Di Luca's positive drug test right before the 2013 Giro d'Italia, one of the biggest races in professional cycling, justifiably revived worries about doping in cycling. Williams asserts that a new generation of synthetic drugs threatens attempts to clean up the sport. One such drug is GW1516, a synthetic drug that functions on a muscle-building gene to allow athletes to train harder and increase their endurance. Williams maintains that although major pharmaceutical companies have agreed to share information about new drugs and new technology with the World Anti-Doping Agency (WADA), the agency still faces a significant challenge in combating new drugs. Richard Williams is a journalist, sportswriter, and author.

As you read, consider the following questions:

1. According to Richard Williams, what banned substance did Danilo Di Luca test positive for during the 2009 Giro d'Italia?

2. When did pharmaceutical giant GlaxoSmithKline drop testing of GW1516, according to Williams?

3. How can the exogenous use of Aicar be detected in an individual athlete's body, according to Williams?

When Danilo Di Luca got himself thrown off the Giro d'Italia a couple of weeks ago, it seemed like a gust of stale air blowing in from a half-forgotten past. Traces of erythropoietin [EPO] had been found in a urine sample given by the 37-year-old Italian rider a few days before the start of the race. Di Luca had form, and plenty of it: his most recent ban had come after tests during the 2009 Giro—a race he had won two years previously—revealed the presence of Cera, a sophisticated form of EPO.

The cycling world was furious with him for reviving the spectre of its tainted history. But perhaps they should be less worried about veteran recidivists indulging in old doping habits than in the possibility of future scandals involving a new generation of drugs.

GW1516

Over the past six months a number of riders have tested positive for GW1516, a synthetic substance which works on a muscle-building gene. It persuades the body to send more oxygen to the muscles by using up fat rather than carbohydrate or protein, which thus remain available to build muscle tissue. Athletes can employ it to train harder and increase their endurance, the classic job of a modern performance-enhancing drug.

It was first synthesised by GlaxoSmithKline [(GSK)], which saw the hugely lucrative potential for marketing it to people wanting to lose weight. But when the company's scientists tested it on rodents, they didn't like what they found. In large doses it induced cancers in various organs of the body, from the tongue and the thyroid to the testes and the ovaries by way of the kidneys and the liver. In 2006, without going any further, GSK dropped it. Yet this is the substance recently revealed to have been detected in samples taken during the Tour of Costa Rica last December from four local professionals—Paulo Vargas Barrantes, Pablo Mudarra Segura and Allan Morales Castillo, all of the BCR Pizza Hut team, and Steven Villalobos Azofeifa of the Coronado team—and from a Colombian rider Marlon Pérez, of the Colombia-Claro team.

Those results were announced in April [2013], which also happened to be the month in which out-of-competition tests in Europe exposed the use of GW1516 by Valery Kaykov, a Russian rider with the RusVelo team, and Miguel Ubeto, a Venezuelan with Lampre-Merida.

A Dangerous Drug

Despite GSK's decision to end their efforts to clear the drug for medical use, others are manufacturing it without medical clearance. A single click reveals GW1516 to be the third highest-selling product on one internet site, at $119 for a 150-mg bottle.

On 21 March, shortly before the GW1516 positives were revealed, the World Anti-Doping Agency [(WADA)] issued a warning against its use. "Clinical approval has not and will not be given for this substance," it said. "The side-effect . . . is so serious that WADA is taking the rare step of warning 'cheats' to ensure that there is complete awareness of the possible health risks to athletes who succumb to the temptation of using (it) for performance enhancement."

Alfredo Martirena/www.CartoonStock.com.

Aicar

Clear enough. But GW1516 has a little friend. This one is
called Aicar, pronounced "ay-car", and it does a similar job

through different means. It is available on the same website, at $98 for 100mg, and the possible side-effects have yet to be publicised. But as Michael Stow, the head of science and medicine at UK Anti-Doping, told me: "We know that dangers exist, predominantly related to its effects on the heart and to levels of lactic and uric acid, which can result in conditions such as gout and arthritis."

Where GW1516 functions on a gene, Aicar sends its message through metabolic pathways, and there is evidence to suggest that some athletes combine the two in a cocktail that enhances the effects of both. And neither has been medically approved.

So is there a real cause for concern? "Yes," Andy Parkinson, UK Anti-Doping's chief executive, said. "We're concerned about athletes using any substances that haven't passed trials with the pharmaceutical companies, and the potential use of gene-doping has got to be a worry."

A Breakthrough Memorandum

It is 18 months since WADA and the major pharmaceutical companies signed a joint memorandum of understanding, under which the industry supplies advance information about their new products to the anti-doping authorities, helping them to devise methods of recognising those falling outside the boundaries of acceptable use in sport.

"The pharma business is a highly competitive one and information on new drugs is commercially sensitive," Parkinson said, "so that was a big step forward." That cooperation led to a detectable "marker" being placed in Cera during the manufacturing process. None of that, however, can regulate what he calls illicit and copycat manufacturing. "We're seeing these things sold on the internet by people who have no regulator. The athletes who buy these products have no idea what they're receiving and putting into their bodies."

Given recent history, it is natural that cycling should come under the spotlight. "But other sports aren't immune," Parkinson said. Although he would not elaborate, it can be assumed that any endurance sport might contain athletes vulnerable to these new temptations.

Keeping Up with Technology

As with previous generations of performance-enhancing drugs, the testers are running to catch up with the cheats. Once the use of EPO had been detected, it took several years to devise adequate tests for a substance that occurs naturally in the human body.

GW1516, which is entirely artificial, can now be spotted with certainty. Identifying the exogenous use of naturally occurring Aicar involves the constant monitoring required by the bio-passport [a record of an athlete's biological markers and drug tests collated over time], where unusual fluctuations in the level of its presence within an individual athlete's body can be logged.

The threat posed to cheats by anti-doping measures is also reinforced by a significant improvement in retesting. "We've got bigger freezers," Parkinson said, "and there's a statute of limitations allowing us to keep them for retesting for up to eight years." A new substance that is hard to spot today might be easy to detect the day after tomorrow.

The cyclists so far found to have used these rogue products are not famous. They are not even the sort of riders to be found at the back of the Tour de France peloton [main group of cyclists in a race]. . . . They might not be the cleverest or more sophisticated users of doping products. Nor are they from a single team, or a single country, or even a single continent. Plenty of room for concern, then, that while the vast majority of cyclists battle to restore their sport's reputation, a delinquent minority is proving hard to budge.

Periodical and Internet Sources Bibliography

The following articles have been selected to supplement the diverse views presented in this chapter.

Tim Carmody	"Hacking Your Body: Lance Armstrong and the Science of Doping," The Verge, January 17, 2013.
Claudio Gatti	"Looking Upstream in Doping Cases," *New York Times*, January 15, 2013.
Nick Gillespie	"The Sports Media's Great Ryan Braun Freak-Out," *The Daily Beast*, July 28, 2013.
Bill Livingston	"Performance-Enhancing Drugs Should Be Legalized in Pro Sports, Olympics," Cleveland.com, July 9, 2013.
Eric Niiler	"Does Athletic Doping Even Work?" *Discovery News*, December 5, 2012.
Darian Nourian	"Doping Affects the Entire Nature of Sports," *Daily Trojan*, January 22, 2013.
Brian Palmer	"The Long-Term Benefits of Juicing," *Slate*, March 30, 2012.
Steven Reinberg	"As Armstrong Case Unfolds, Experts Describe Doping's Harms," *U.S. News & World Report*, October 11, 2012.
Jeremy Rozansky	"How to Think of Our Steroid Superman," *New Atlantis*, January 19, 2013.
Helen Thompson	"Performance Enhancement: Superhuman Athletes," *Nature*, July 18, 2012.
Bill Wilson	"The Real Cost of Doping in Sport," *BBC News*, March 15, 2012.

CHAPTER 2

Should Doping Be Banned?

Chapter Preface

In 1928 the International Association of Athletics Federations (IAAF) established the first antidoping ban. The ban applied to any substance that could stimulate physical performance. In the early twentieth century, this ban focused on substances such as alcohol, caffeine, cocaine, herbal potions, and strychnine (a poison that acts as a stimulant to the nervous system in small doses). However, there was no way to test for banned substances, so athletes violated the doping ban, which was adopted by many other international sporting federations by the mid-twentieth century.

By the 1930s, the development of and increased access to synthetic hormones and amphetamines signaled a new era for doping in sports. Historians contend that the use of *pot Belge*, a mixture of drugs that can include amphetamines, caffeine, heroin, and cocaine, became common in cycling races around that same time, especially in the Tour de France, a famous cycling race that takes place every year in France and neighboring countries. Despite the concern over the spread of doping in many major sports, international athletic federations were ineffective in addressing the problem.

The death of Danish cyclist Knud Enemark Jensen during the 100m team time trials at the 1960 Olympics was a turning point for Olympic competition. An autopsy later determined that Jensen had traces of several banned substances in his blood, including amphetamine. Jensen's death shocked the sporting world and increased the pressure on international athletic federations to introduce a system for drug testing.

In 1966 the International Cycling Union and the Fédération Internationale de Football Association, the international soccer federation, both introduced drug testing in their respective World Championships. For the first time athletes were being tested for banned substances. A year later the International Olympic Committee (IOC) created its first prohibited-substances list and instituted a medical committee to oversee its antidoping program. In 1968 a system of drug testing was implemented at both the summer and winter Olympic Games. At the 1972 Olympics in Munich, Germany, officials conducted more than two thousand urine tests; there were nine positive results.

The development of anabolic steroids was another challenge for international sports federations. Anabolic steroids were particularly popular with athletes in strength sports, like weightlifting, and were widespread until a reliable testing method was put in place in 1974. The IOC added anabolic steroids to its prohibited-substance list in 1976.

During the 1970s and 1980s, systematic doping regimens in several Soviet bloc countries posed problems for the IOC and other international athletic federations. Some countries, such as East Germany, practiced a state-sponsored, institutionalized strategy to dope its athletes to compete and win international sports competitions, including the Olympics. They employed the best doctors to find ways to mask doping agents and avoid detection.

Several high-profile cases of doping in sports in the 1980s put pressure on international athletic organizations to develop more effective and sophisticated testing methods. When these improved tests were employed in the 1990s, there were dramatic results in several sports.

There were always new challenges to face. Erythropoietin (EPO), a synthetic hormone that increases the flow of oxygen to the muscles, was banned in 1990; however, an effective test was not implemented until the 2000 Olympics. By that time, EPO use had become endemic in cycling.

A new era in antidoping efforts emerged in the late twentieth and early twenty-first centuries, as international cooperation to combat doping in sports dramatically improved. The founding of the World Anti-Doping Agency (WADA) in 1999 made a huge difference. WADA is an independent agency tasked with setting standards for antidoping programs and coordinating antidoping efforts between athletes, various government agencies, international sporting federations, and international agencies.

This chapter explores the question of whether doping should be banned in sports. The viewpoints presented debate the efficacy and ethics of antidoping efforts and the implications of allowing athletes to use performance-enhancing drugs.

> *"In a culture that encourages the constant search for the limits of human achievement, we, the consumers of popular sports entertainment, revel in record-breaking, gravity-defying, barely believable feats on the field of play."*

Doping Should Be Allowed

Ellis Cashmore

In the following viewpoint, Ellis Cashmore argues that doping should be allowed in sports and that if it is, it should be transparent and monitored by responsible medical personnel. Cashmore points out that despite bans and harsh penalties, doping continues in sports and most users remain undetected. He concludes that it is naive to expect that doping can be eliminated completely; therefore, allowing it is a practical solution to doping in sports. Ellis Cashmore is an author and a professor of culture, media, and sport at Staffordshire University in England.

As you read, consider the following questions:

1. According to Ellis Cashmore, in what year was Ben Johnson disqualified from the Olympics for testing positive for drugs?

2. How much money does the Cashmore say that Lance Armstrong is worth?

3. According to Ellis Cashmore, what event did Marion Jones win at the 2000 Olympic Games?

The Lance Armstrong case [sports officials determined that the American cyclist had used performance-enhancing drugs] forces us to consider a philosophical problem that has tormented sport since 1988 when [Canadian sprinter] Ben Johnson was disqualified from the Olympics after testing positive for drugs.

Asking the Right Question

Not "How we can improve detection and make punishment serve as both deterrent and restitution," but "Should we allow athletes to use drugs?" My answer is yes.

Were we to treat athletes as mature adults capable of making informed decisions based on scientific information, we could permit the use of performance enhancing substances, monitor the results and make the whole process transparent.

Instead we continue to demonize those found guilty of doping violations, willing ourselves into ignorance.

Athletes take unknown substances, procured from unknown sources and with uncertain results. Permitting the use of doping would rescue sport from this clandestine state, creating an environment that would be not only safer, but more congruent with the reality of professional sport in the 21st century.

Twenty-four years after the Johnson scandal, performance-enhancing drugs are as abundant as ever and, as the Armstrong experience reminds us, the testers remain embarrassingly behind the curve. Despite the major advances since 1988, several athletes have evaded detection not just for the odd competition, but for entire careers.

Before Armstrong, American sprinter Marion Jones was convicted and imprisoned, though, like Armstrong, she never returned a positive drug test (she was found guilty of impeding a Federal investigation). Nor did [American baseball player] Barry Bonds, who was convicted on one count of misleading a grand jury investigating drug use by athletes in 2011.

A High-Stakes Career

No sensible observer of sport today denies the prevalence of drugs in practically every major sport, yet none would argue they can ever be eliminated completely. Money alone guarantees that much. The days of the gentleman-amateur have long gone: Athletes today are competing for high stakes, not just millions, but dozens of millions (Armstrong is worth about $70 million, according to *Forbes* [magazine]).

In a culture that encourages the constant search for the limits of human achievement, we, the consumers of popular sports entertainment, revel in record-breaking, gravity-defying, barely believable feats on the field of play. Promoters, leagues, sponsors, advertisers and a miscellany of other interested parties dangle incentives.

Armstrong got rich thanks to the beneficence of people who didn't just back him but lauded, even lionized him as the greatest cyclist ever, and perhaps pound-for-pound one of the world's finest sportsmen. Small wonder he was motivated to gamble: a quick cost-benefit calculation would have told him the chances of detection were slight compared with the bounties available.

Reviewing the Objections

The objections are predictable:

This is cheating. In a technical sense, perhaps; but that could be fixed by changing the rules. In a moral sense, it is unfair on those competitors who do not wish to use drugs.

The Fall of Ben Johnson

Canadian sprinter Ben Johnson ... was expected to win gold in the 100 meters at the 1988 Olympics in Seoul, Korea. He did win, setting a new record with an amazing time of 9.79 seconds. But when he was tested for drugs authorities found traces of an anabolic steroid, stanozolol, in his urine. Johnson was stripped of his gold medal, which went to [Carl] Lewis, who had come in second. In addition, he was suspended from competition for two years. Johnson denied having taken drugs for some time, until [his coach and trainer Charles] Francis testified in court that Johnson had been using them. Johnson finally admitted that he had been taking drugs since 1981, making all his previous achievements seem questionable.

Johnson lost all his endorsement contracts, and officials considered stripping him of his 1987 Rome victory [in the 100-meter World Championships in Italy]. Francis testified in 1989 that Johnson had indeed taken steroids before setting his Rome world record. In 1989, the International Amateur Athletic Foundation passed a resolution stating that as of January 1, 1990, Johnson's previous world records would be declared invalid. ...

In 1990, Johnson was reinstated to Olympic competition. He began working with a new coach, Loren Seagrave, and planned to compete in the 1992 Olympics in Barcelona. ... In January of 1992, Johnson competed in a Montreal track meet, where he was tested for drugs and found to be using testosterone. As a result, the International Amateur Athletic Foundation slapped him with a lifetime ban from competition.

"Ben Johnson," Biography in Context Online Collection, *Detroit, MI: Gale, 2013.*

The evidence of the Armstrong investigation suggests that many other cyclists were habitual dopers, anyway. We can't say the same for other sports, though we can remind competitors that among the array of performance enhancing aids which are available to them, such as acupuncture, hypnotism, hypoxic tents (that simulate high altitude) and the countless other perfectly legal performance enhancements are some that are probably more dangerous than drugs.

Taking drugs is wrong. Maybe, but how many of us get through a day without taking a pharmaceutical product, such as statins, antidepressants, painkillers and so on? By an accident of language we use the same term for these products and performance enhancing materials as we do for illicit drugs like crack cocaine and heroin. This misleads us into imagining related objections.

There are too many dangers. Of course there are—as the situation is now. By inviting athletes to declare with impunity what they are using, we encourage and open discourse and promote research so we'd be in a position to advise on the relative values and risks of different substances. This openness isn't possible while we continue to force drug-taking underground. Opening up sport in the way I'm advocating would render it a safer, more secure environment.

Sports stars are role models. Possibly. But they are not paragons of virtue, and even if they were, young people who follow them and organize their own naive ambitions around theirs will eventually run into the rock hard reality that drugs are to sport what Twitter is to celebrities—not exactly essential, but a valuable resource when used strategically.

Fans would turn off sport. Ask yourself this: Did you feel a thrill when you saw the imperious Armstrong cross the line at the 2002 Tour de France seven minutes ahead of his nearest rival? Or when you watched Marion Jones surge to victory at the Olympic 100m final in 2000? At the time, we didn't realize they or, for that matter, any of their rivals had doped. And it didn't affect our enjoyment of their performances any more than if we'd known they were wearing aerodynamically designed clothing.

The argument in favour of permitting drugs in sport is not popular at a time when the world is busy annihilating Lance Armstrong. But it is rational, sound and in harmony with sport, not as it was in the days of *Chariots of Fire* [a movie based on the true story of two athletes competing in the 1924 Olympics], but as it is in the twenty first century: Unrelenting, mercilessly competitive and unsparingly achievement-oriented.

> "Wherever the line is drawn, some ath-
> letes will venture to the other side."

Doping Should Be Banned

Tom Murray

In the following viewpoint, Tom Murray contends that allowing doping in sports violates two essential truths about sport: One, athletes are so competitive that some will break the rules, and two, rules are necessary. Murray further argues that the point of sports is to compete and excel within certain rules—even if they seem arbitrary or old-fashioned. Tom Murray is president emeritus of the Hastings Center, a nonprofit research institute in New York, and chair of the Ethical Issues Expert Group of the World Anti-Doping Agency.

As you read, consider the following questions:

1. According to Tom Murray, how many framed Tour de France jerseys does Lance Armstrong own?

2. What kind of advantage does drugs and blood transfusion provide to athletes, according to Murray?

3. Why is a baseball pitcher's rubber 60 feet, 6 inches from home plate, according to Murray?

Day after day, it seems, more top cyclists who competed in the sport's peak doping era are admitting they broke the rules. The cult of omerta [code of silence] has at last been broken; Lance Armstrong's supporters are running out of plausible defenses. His recent photo of himself reclining in front of his seven framed Tour de France jerseys is more sad than defiant: He's been stripped of the championship titles they once represented. The facts laid out in the U.S. Anti-Doping Agency's decision and the affidavits by his former teammates cut off just about every avenue of escape.

Except one. Some critics say the problem isn't athletes who break the rules but the rules themselves—specifically, the prohibition on doping. They argue that using performance-enhancing technologies such as the blood-boosting hormone EPO [erythropoietin], testosterone and blood transfusions would not be cheating if they were not prohibited. True. Some even celebrate athletes transformed by technology. But these critics don't understand two essential truths about sport.

A Difficult Choice

Statements by cyclists such as [American] Dave Zabriskie or [American] Tyler Hamilton, in his book *The Secret Race*, help clarify the stakes. More than 30 years of conversations with elite athletes have made clear to me what happens: Exceptionally talented young athletes rise through the ranks, eager to reach the top. Some get tantalizingly close, only to discover that success and acceptance mean doing what their competitors are doing.

For a sad era in cycling, from the late 1980s to 2008, it meant doping. Mr. Hamilton described a grooming process: Once he was offered one of the drug-filled "white bags" that team leaders were given, it was a sign that he'd arrived. Other cyclists have described pressures to conform to the team leader's demands. For the U.S. Postal Service team, that often meant paying for the services of the notorious Italian physician and doping expert Michele Ferrari.

The math is straightforward. The difference between standing on the [winner's] podium and straggling in with the peloton [main group of cyclists in a race] may be 1 percent in terms of performance. When drugs and blood transfusions provide a 5 percent advantage, athletes who refuse to dope when others do are making a choice. It's an honorable choice, but it diminishes their hope of winning or simply staying on a team.

The first hard truth about elite sport is that its relentless competitiveness, and the tiny margins that separate winners from also-rans, press athletes not to surrender anything that gives them an edge. If the skeptics had their way, any permissible thing that provided an advantage—hormone injections, transfusions and more—would immediately become the absolute minimum for all serious elite athletes in a given sport. And there is no reason to believe athletes would stop there. Wherever the line is drawn, some athletes will venture to the other side.

The doubters have to make a choice. Either everything will be allowed, probably with serious consequences for the health of elite athletes and those who aspire to be like them, or some forms of doping will continue to be banned, which means there will still be rules to be monitored, enforced—and broken.

The Importance of Rules

The second truth about sport is more fundamental. Any thoughtful person who plays a sport understands the connection among talent, dedication and excellence. Every sport sets limits (with the possible exception of Calvinball, whose only rule is that you can't have the same rules twice). Professional golfers are not allowed to use clubs that make it easy to hit out of the rough or balls that fly straight rather than hooking or slicing. Major leaguers must use wooden, not metal, bats. Sports don't make it easy.

Some rules seem especially arbitrary. A baseball pitcher's rubber [a white, rubber slab on the pitcher's mound] is 60 feet 6 inches from home plate. Why? Because it works. Because it sustains the wonderful tension between pitcher and batter, even if adjustments have to be made to the size of the strike zone or the height of the mound (as in 1968, when pitchers such as Bob Gibson and Don Drysdale dominated). When the rules of a sport are grounded in whatever varieties of excellence that particular sport values, they're not arbitrary in a bad way. In fact, they're necessary.

I'm an amateur cyclist. I don't race, but I do set challenges for myself. Would injections of the hormone EPO or blood transfusions allow me to go faster and farther? Sure. An electric motor on my bike would work even better. But what's the point?

The meaning of cycling, like the meaning of every sport worth the name, is in the values it fosters, the particular forms of human excellence it exhibits and the dedication each individual shows in perfecting his or her natural talents. The rules against doping remind us what's valuable about sport. They help us remember why we play.

"The science of drug testing has progressed, but it appears that the dopers are always a step ahead."

Legalise Doping or Lose the Spectacle of Sport

Julian Savulescu

In the following viewpoint, written in July 2013, Julian Savulescu suggests that the zero-balance policy currently in place for doping in sport is not working: Dopers are always a step ahead of the testing process, and athletes will always be tempted to use performance-enhancing drugs (PEDs) to get a competitive edge. Savulescu proposes that doping be legalized but strictly regulated so PEDs could be administered safely by qualified medical personnel. Savulescu concludes that athletes should have the right to optimize their own physiology without overriding the value of the sport. Julian Savulescu is the director of the Uehiro Centre for Practical Ethics, the Oxford Centre for Neuroethics, and the Institute for Science and Ethics at Oxford University in England.

As you read, consider the following questions:

1. According to Julian Savulescu, how many Turkish athletes tested positive for performance-enhancing drugs in the first half of 2013?

2. When were the first tests for EPO introduced, according to Savulescu?

3. According to Savulescu, which athlete was banned from his sport for life following a positive drug test in 2011?

Sport, at both international and local levels, seems to constantly be in a doping crisis. It may be time to consider legalising performance enhancers because zero tolerance is clearly not working.

This week, the second-fastest runner of all time, Tyson Gay, reportedly tested positive for a banned substance, along with the Jamaican sprinters Asafa Powell, and Sherone Simpson, making for shocked headlines across the world.

And this is just one such high-profile story across numerous sports and countries. In athletics, 24 Turkish athletes are confirmed to have tested positive this year; Australian Rules Football is still reeling from the ongoing Essendon scandal; and over in the United States, inquiries into an anti-ageing laboratory said to supply human growth hormone to top baseball players continues.

While the 100th Tour de France is so far untainted by positive tests, cycling doping cases have continued this year with two Giro D'Italia riders testing positive.

But there's still a sense that we are just seeing the tip of the iceberg. Cyclist Chris Froome, who is now tested at the end of each Tour de France stage as the yellow jersey, has been relentlessly hounded over whether his recent impressive performances are due to doping.

The Failure of Zero Tolerance

We don't know who is doping and who is not. What we do know is that the zero tolerance ban on doping has failed.

The "war on doping" has seen several false victories. In 2000, the first tests for the substance EPO were introduced. (EPO is short for erythropoietin, which is a naturally occurring hormone found in the blood, athletes use the artificial peptide recombinant EPO to stimulate red blood cell production for improving oxygen transfer and boosting endurance or recovery from anaerobic exercise.)

In 2007, Pat McQuaid, head of Union Cycliste Internationale (the cycling association that oversees competitive cycling events internationally), declared biological passports "a new and historic step in the fight against doping."

Autologous blood tests were all but announced for the 2012 Olympics, but have apparently still not been implemented.

The science of drug testing has progressed, but it appears that the dopers are always a step ahead.

Lance Armstrong is a case in point. He was tested in competition and out of competition, before and after EPO tests were implemented and before and after biological passports were introduced.

But he was only caught through the forced testimony of his teammates, who turned him in for the chance to continue their own careers as confessed dopers. And many of them are still riding at the elite, professional level.

The decision of the Spanish court to destroy evidence from the trial of Eufemiano Fuentes (a sports doctor found guilty of providing cyclists with blood doping) means we may never know who was involved with that particular clinic.

But it is thought to include clients from athletics, tennis and football as well as cyclists.

Leading expert on performance-enhancing drugs Werner Franke pointed out just before the last Olympics that half of

Erythropoietin

EPO [erythropoietin] and other forms of blood doping improve athletic performance by increasing the number of red blood cells in the body. Red blood cells carry oxygen to muscles and increase their performance. EPO and other forms of blood doping, therefore, increase the athlete's aerobic capacity and endurance. Originally, blood doping involved blood transfusions using blood with increased red blood cell counts. The red blood cell–enriched blood, often the athlete's own blood, would be injected into the athlete before an event. Although traditional blood doping is still used, most blood doping today uses synthetic EPO, a hormone that increases the production of red blood cells. EPO occurs naturally in the body, but scientists developed a synthetic version of EPO in the late 1980s. Blood doping can lead to polycythemia, a condition in which the blood thickens because red blood cell counts are abnormally high. Polycythemia can lead to stroke or cardiac arrest. The use of EPO and blood doping is most common in endurance sports, such as cycling, marathons, and cross-country skiing.

"Sports and Drug Use,"
Global Issues in Context Online Collection.
Detroit, MI: Gale, 2013.

the men's 100-metre finalists in two previous Olympics were later reported to have been doping.

Less than a year after London 2012, if Gay and Powell's tests are confirmed, we will be half way to the same level at the 2012 final. A third member of the eight-man line up, Justin Gaitlin, was previously banned for doping.

Time and again, we are told the culture has changed. But the doping cases keep coming, and performances keep improving. The 2012 Olympics saw 66 Olympic records and 30 world records broken.

The Limits of Human Physiology

We reached the limits of human performance in sprinting about 15 years ago; the limit for a man running 100 metres seems to be about 9.7 seconds. Ben Johnson ran that distance in 9.79 seconds in 1988 but was doping.

In 2005, American Tim Montgomery, a former 100-metre world-record holder was banned for doping after running 9.78 seconds in 2002. In 2006, Justin Gatlin, the defending 100-metre Olympic champion, was banned for doping three weeks after equalling the world record (9.77 seconds at the time).

In 2009, Jamaican Yohan Blake got a three-month ban for doping. Two years later, he became world champion in the 100-metre sprint and won a silver medal in the last Olympics. He co-owns the second-fastest time in history alongside the recently banned Tyson Gay (9.69 seconds).

In 2011, Steve Mullings of Jamaica was hit with a lifetime ban following a positive test for a masking product after having run a personal best 9.8 seconds.

It seems that if you are running 100 metres in around 9.7 seconds, you are likely to be taking performance enhancers.

To keep improving, to keep beating records, to continue to train at the peak of fitness, to recover from the injury that training inflicts, we need enhanced physiology.

Spectators want faster times and broken records, so do athletes. But we have exhausted the human potential.

Is it wrong to aim for zero tolerance and performances that are within natural human limits? No, but it is not enforceable.

What About Safety?

The strongest argument against doping is safety. But anything is dangerous if taken to excess; water will kill you if you drink enough of it.

Over the last 20 years, sport has shown that performance enhancers can be administered safely. They could be administered even more safely if doping was brought out into the open.

Of course there is no such thing as risk-free sport. But we need a balance between safety, enforceability, and spectacle.

Consider cycling competitions.

They show that elite sport is fundamentally unsafe, as Team Sky's Edvald Boassen Hagen and Geraint Thomas, both nursing fractures from recent cycling crashes, can tell you.

It was entirely appropriate to enforce the wearing of helmets to limit the safety risks. But it would be inappropriate to limit the race to only straight, wide roads, or to remove downhill racing or to take any number of other measures that would increase safety but ruin the sport as a spectacle and as a cultural practice.

It would be a waste of time to take other measures, such as limiting the amount of time or the speed that riders can train at, even on the grounds of safety. It could not be enforced.

Enforceability requires a reasonable limits. If we set the maximum speed limit for cars to 20 kilometres an hour, it would be safer. Many, perhaps most of the people who died on the roads in any given year would be saved. But more people would speed.

We need to find a workable, enforceable balance.

The Right Limits

A second, good objection lies in the nature of the intervention. If a substance came to dominate the sport and override its value, that would be a good reason to ban it.

If boxers could feel no fear, for instance, or if archers could be given rock steady hands, it should be impermissible. But if a substance allows safer, faster recovery from training, or from injury, then it does not interfere with the sport.

We are confused, and often emotional, about doping. The word drugs brings to mind substances such as ecstasy or cocaine or heroin. But most doping today uses natural substances that are involved in normal human physiology and naturally vary from time to time and person to person.

Testosterone, blood, and growth hormone are all endogenous substances (that occur naturally within the body), which are banned. While drugs such as caffeine are exogenous (not naturally occurring in the body) and effective in increasing performance, but allowed.

Taking the drug EPO increases hematocrit (ratio of red blood cells to total blood volume) levels, and is banned. Sleeping in a hypoxic air tent has the same effect, but is perfectly legal.

Athletes are using these substances to optimise their own physiology, just as they do with diet, trying to maximise fluids and glucose at the right times. Confessed doping cyclist Tyler Hamilton claims to have lost a race due to failing to take a 100-calorie energy gel at the correct time (despite the fact he was also doping) in his book *The Secret Race*.

All of these variables are themselves affected by training at elite levels. Over the course of the Tour de France, a cyclist would lose their natural levels of red blood cells from the immense effort.

Training is about optimising human physiology, whether by changing the diet to influence the availability of glucose and glycogen, or by taking EPO in order to increase the availability of oxygen.

The risks of doping have been overstated, and zero-tolerance represents the kind of unreasonable limit that is destined to be ignored by athletes. It's time to rethink the absolute ban and instead to pick limits that are safe and enforceable.

> *"Allowing for the regulated use of performance-enhancing drugs does not stop the arms race of doping among athletes, but only sanctions it."*

The Legalization of Doping Would Sanction an Escalation in Drug Use

James H. Hibbard

In the following viewpoint, James H. Hibbard maintains that the growing movement to legalize and regulate the use of performance-enhancing drugs (PEDs) among athletes is fundamentally wrong. He argues that allowing the use of PEDs would mean that even more athletes would dope, setting off an escalation in PED use. Hibbard also contends that if PEDs were allowed, athletes would just turn to other, unproven, and potentially dangerous drugs to gain a competitive advantage. Hibbard concludes that legalizing and regulating PEDs will not make sports safer or create fairer competition. James H. Hibbard is a former professional cyclist. He studied philosophy at the University of California, Santa Cruz and at DePaul University in Chicago, Illinois.

As you read, consider the following questions:

1. When did the Festina affair occur, according to James H. Hibbard?

2. What author does Hibbard identify as an influential voice in the movement to regulate performance-enhancing drugs?

3. According to Hibbard, what fiction are almost all justifications for the allowance of performance-enhancing drugs predicated upon?

Since the so-caled "Festina Scandal" at the 1998 Tour de France which exposed team-wide systematic doping for the first time in modern cycling, professional road cycling has been besieged by a series of doping cases which have deeply undermined the credibility of the sport. The list of doping cases over the last decade-and-half [1995–2010] reads like a who's who of cycling and includes grand-tour winners like Floyd Landis, Jan Ullrich, Alberto Contador, and of course, Lance Armstrong. Nearly every cyclist who has achieved sufficient professional success to become a household name in the last fifteen years has either been implicated in a doping scandal, or outright tested positive for banned substances.

How does professional cycling best address the problem of its own credibility? And moreover, is "credibility" even a concept that squares well with the lucrative and hypercompetitive nature of sports in the 21st century?

Legalizing PEDs

At first glance, the obvious answer as to how to address cycling's "credibility" problem would appear to be more rigorous testing methods and harsher sanctions, but a vocal minority has also proposed the radical option of legalizing the use of performance-enhancing drugs (PEDs). The logic goes that if athletes are mere entertainers, why not simply allow doping in the professional ranks and cease to frame the question of doping in moral terms. After years of scandal, it takes very little rationalizing to simply give up on concepts of "credibility," to stop looking for "fair" outcomes in sports, and to simply say "Let them dope."

Paramount among doping scandals in cycling is of course the case of Lance Armstrong who in January 2013 confessed to having used performance-enhancing drugs in order to win all seven of his Tour de France titles (and hinted that his use of PEDs even predated his first Tour de France victory). However, there is nothing fundamentally novel about Armstrong's case, other than the magnitude of his fraud and the scope of his deception. In the aftermath of Armstrong's admission, some commentators have called for a cathartic period of amnesty for those who confess to their past use of performance-enhancing drugs and have proposed some form of a truth and reconciliation panel. However, others have used the Armstrong case as further evidence that the use of performance-enhancing drugs is so pervasive—Armstrong likened taking drugs to an occurrence as regular as pumping one's tires—that the only viable way to address the problem is to allow the regulated use of PEDs amongst professional riders.

Proponents for allowing the use of performance-enhancing drugs tend to base their position on three fundamental claims. First, that the numerous scandals have revealed the problem of doping to be so endemic that anti-doping measures will always lag behind the drugs and methods employed by athletes, and that it is therefore best to simply acknowledge that professional athletes dope.

Secondly, that if the use of performance-enhancing drugs were to be allowed, it would be possible to regulate and impose safety standards for the use of performance-enhancing drugs by athletes who, because of current anti-doping regulations, often employ dangerous doping regimens administered with minimal medical oversight.

And finally that doping would yield the same results—just on a higher plane. The most physically talented athlete who is doped will still beat out less talented athletes who are likewise using drugs.

Support for Legalization of PEDs

One of those who argues for the regulation of performance-enhancing drugs is *Freakonomics* co-author Stephen J. Dubner. In 2007, shortly after the conclusion of yet another Tour de France marred by doping scandals, Dubner suggested in his *New York Times* piece, "Should We Just Let the Tour de France Dopers Dope Away?" that regulated doping should be considered. As Dubner wrote,

> Is it time, perhaps, to come up with a pre-approved list of performance-enhancing agents and procedures, require the riders to accept full responsibility for whatever long-term physical and emotional damage these agents and procedures may produce, and let everyone ride on a relatively even keel without having to ban the leader every third day? If the cyclists are already doping, why should we worry about their health? If the sport is already so gravely compromised, why should we pretend it hasn't been?

Another who believes that the way forward is legalization is *Forbes* [magazine's sportswriter] Chris Smith who in his 2013 article "Why It's Time to Legalize Steroids in Professional Sports," takes a slightly different tact from Dubner claiming,

> So if we really want to level the playing field, it may be time to head in the other direction: legalize performance enhancers. Not only would the playing field suddenly be even for all players, it would be at a higher level. A huge part of watching sports is witnessing the very peak of human athletic ability, and legalizing performance-enhancing drugs would help athletes climb even higher. Steroids and doping will help pitchers to throw harder, home runs to go further, cyclists to charge for longer and sprinters to test the very limits of human speed.

While no sports organizations or governing bodies have publicly given any indication that they are considering any such proposal, it is worth thinking about what is at stake in the debate over performance-enhancing drugs, and why those who say "let them dope" risk robbing professional sports of very elements that make them engaging and significant.

The Doping Race

Doping is neither universal, nor does it take place in a closed system among a participant pool of athletes with no turnover. However, both of these beliefs are latent in Dubner's claim that ". . . the cyclists are already doping. . . ." In the assertion that there is a monolithic group of "cyclists", and that this group of individuals has made an informed decision to use performance-enhancing drugs, Dubner ignores the vicious turnover that is part of professional sports, and what allowing for the use of performance-enhancing drugs would mean for every athlete who aspires to break into the professional ranks.

In the wake of those who have elected to dope are numerous other athletes who have either continued competing at a lower level without drugs, or who have left the sport entirely. If doping were to be allowed, rising to the highest levels of sport becomes contingent not upon only hard work, talent, and perseverance, but also upon an athlete's willingness to take risks with their health.

Also implicit in the argument for legalizing doping is the belief that doing so will as Chris Smith claims, "level the proverbial playing field." That is, that once everyone is allowed to dope in some sort of a "standardized" fashion the results will somehow once again be fair—simply elevated to a new plane of performance upon a universal rising tide. The logic seems to be that if a given rider is five percent better than his peers naturally, that once he and the rest of his competitors engage in the same sanctioned doping regimen, this same rider will still be five percent better than his peers. However, when this claim is examined, both the science and means of ground-level implementation are far less clear-cut.

Problems with Standardizing

An illustrative example of the difficulties of "standardizing" doping is hematocrit—a measure of the percentage of one's volume of whole blood that is composed of red blood cells. Critically for endurance sports, hematocrit helps to inform how much oxygen can be carried to working muscles. As a result, raising one's hematocrit (and hence one's aerobic capacity) is frequently the aim of both drugs such as EPO, and illegal methods like blood transfusions.

If one has a high hematocrit one will likely be able to perform better at endurance sports such as cycling. Thus, to follow out the logic of legalizing doping, it would have to be decided from the outset if "doping to level the playing field" means increasing every relevant physiological parameter by a certain percentage from an individual's baseline, or simply raising athlete's hematocrit (or other relevant parameter) to a pre-determined level. If doping means the former—namely increasing baseline levels by fixed percentages so as to maintain genetic differences—one again bumps up against issues of safety and health, as those who naturally have a high hematocrit can only increase it so much without thickening their blood to such an extent that they risk heart attack. This discussion may appear to be a digression but it serves to highlight both the practical problems and ethical murkiness that quickly appear as soon as one examines the consequences of legalizing PEDs.

What of the issue of athlete health? While some claim that allowing for the use of performance-enhancing drugs would allow for greater medical oversight, (which ostensibly would mitigate the health risks posed to athletes) any such claim is contingent upon the assumption that the medically safe level of a performance enhancer is the same as the level to yield the

The Floyd Landis Controversy

After the early stages of the 2006 Tour de France, [American cyclist Floyd] Landis, 30, was in position to become the third U.S. champion of the event after seven-time champion Lance Armstrong, who had retired a year earlier, and American Greg LeMond. But while climbing the arduous Alp mountain La Toussuire on July 20 during Stage 17—three days from the finale—Landis "cracked like Humpty Dumpty," Austin Murphy wrote in *Sports Illustrated*. Landis fell to 11th.

Landis and his Phonak teammates devised a plan the next day to bring the rider back within range of the lead—a "Hail Mary pass," as Murphy called it. The Phonak group sprung Landis loose from the riding pack. Landis ended the day third and surged to victory along the Champs-Élysées in Paris on July 23. Murphy called Landis's victory—ironically, given subsequent events—"a gleaming counterweight to the doping scandal that had overshadowed this Tour since the day before it began." Pre-race favorites Ivan Basso and Jan Ullrich, among others, had been banned from the event.

Doubt, however, surrounded the Landis triumph when four days after the race, his team said he had tested for high testosterone levels the day of his comeback. The International Cycling Union, the governing body for the sport, announced August 5 that the backup, or "B" sample, confirmed the testosterone level and said a synthetic hormone was found in his system. "It officially turned a feel-good tale of achievement against long odds into a horror movie for Landis, his supporters, and cycling fans," Bonnie DeSimone wrote in the *Boston Globe*.

"Floyd Landis," Biography in Context Online Collection. *Detroit, MI: Gale, 2010.*

greatest performance gain and that this level is the same for every individual. Allowing for the regulated use of performance-enhancing drugs does not stop the arms race of doping among athletes, but only sanctions it. If a formerly banned substance were to be allowed at a particular level (which is lower than that at which one can maximize one's performance) one can almost be certain that there will be an athlete willing to take the risk of using the substance not at the regulated medically safe level, but rather at a level sufficient to yield the greatest competitive advantage.

Doping Devalues Athletic Achievement

There will always be champions and also-rans, but doping makes it impossible to discern one group from the other. In endurance sports, a new generation of blood-boosting drugs have made champions out of those who, but for their willingness to risk their health, and cheat their competitors, would have never have had the ability to win. And more critically, those who would otherwise have risen to the top of the sport through their natural talent and drive, but who were unwilling to use performance-enhancing drugs, will likely never know what they could have achieved.

Almost all justifications for the allowance of performance-enhancing drugs are predicated upon the fiction that athletes are not like everyone else. Implicit in these justifications is the belief that neither we nor our children would wish or be able to become professional athletes, and that when an athlete elects to use performance-enhancing drugs, he or she is already an adult, competing against other adults, who have made the choice to become professional athletes, fully cognizant of the psychological and physical risks that are necessary in order to rise to the top of his or her chosen profession, but like much of life the situation is nowhere near this tidy.

Athletes *are* like us. And it is because of our ability to sympathize with their successes and failures that sports have any meaning at all. This meaning evaporates though when the collective frustration with doping turns athletes into a monolithic "other," who can use performance-enhancing drugs if they so choose, and whose struggles thus become not like our own, but those of someone unlike anyone whom we would aspire to be.

> *"By walking away from the war on dop-*
> *ing in sport because it appears to be all*
> *too difficult is simply not acceptable."*

We Can't Stop Doping in Sport, So Why Not Give Up?

Glenn Mitchell

In the following viewpoint, Glenn Mitchell asserts that legalizing doping is illogical and violates society's moral code. He further contends that society has a responsibility to protect athletes from using untested and potentially dangerous drugs prescribed by unscrupulous doctors. He writes that the biggest danger is to second-tier professional athletes, because they are not being monitored by medical staff and often self-medicate to enhance their physical performance. Mitchell concludes that society should continue to fight against doping. Glenn Mitchell is a freelance writer, columnist, on-air contributor to radio and television sports shows, and a former sports broadcaster.

As you read, consider the following questions:

1. What US agency uncovered Lance Armstrong's doping, according to Glenn Mitchell?

2. What antiobesity drug does Mitchell identify as a uncertified substance being given to Australian athletes?

3. According to Mitchell, how were synthetic EPO, synthesized testosterone, and anabolic steroids created?

From the contrite and seemingly stage-managed confession by Lance Armstrong to the current allegations swirling around the AFL and NRL, the issue of drugs in sport has not been too far from the headlines of late.

Interestingly, Armstrong's ultimate fall from grace came about not as a result of any specific positive tests but on the back of a long and exhaustive investigation undertaken by the United States Anti-Doping Authority.

Likewise, if there are definitive guilty verdicts handed down with regard to the ASADA investigations into practices within the AFL and NRL, they will have been driven in large part by the year-long investigative operation conducted by the ACC.

Like Marion Jones and the Festina affair and Operación Puerto in cycling, it is not drug testing that is primarily unearthing athletes who are doping but law enforcement and customs investigations.

With so many athletes seemingly evading drug tests successfully, yet subsequently being found guilty of doping through investigative undertakings, many are saying it is perhaps time to admit the battle against doping in sport cannot be won and the continued expenditure of millions of dollars trying to do so is simply a waste.

In short, there are plenty of people who believe the doors should be thrown open, allowing athletes open slather to enhance their performance in any way they see fit.

Scrap the WADA Code and its long list of banned substances and methods with regard to doping and say at all levels of sport anything goes.

Such a theory is ridiculous, and indeed is heavily flawed "logic" that if taken up could have dire consequences for athletes and their families.

By walking away from the war on doping in sport because it appears to be all too difficult is simply not acceptable.

Imagine if, as a society, we adopted the same philosophy when it came to the illicit drugs which are so readily dealt and consumed in the Australian community.

If there were no laws attached to the supply and use of illicit street substances what sort of impact would that have on general society?

Just as we would never contemplate such an approach when it comes to illicit societal drugs, we should seek to stay the course as well when it comes to doping in the sporting realm.

At present, and this has been the case since drug testing in sport became an issue in the late-1960s, a portion of the drugs of choice at any given time are able to be utilised without fear of detection.

Some performance enhancers are actually being given to athletes before they have been granted the certification by regulatory bodies with regard to being fit for human use—the anti-obesity drug AOD-9064, which has been allegedly used in Australia by sports scientists, is one such substance to have recently fallen into that category.

Elite athletes being used as mere guinea pigs is a ghoulish thought.

The use of drugs yet to be regulated for human use are very much in the minority however when it comes to those used in sport.

Almost without fail, the drugs that have been used unethically in sport have been invented as a result of medical and pharmaceutical research that is endeavouring to help patients overcome medical conditions.

The birth of synthetic EPO, synthesized testosterone and anabolic steroids all came about as a result of research done with respect to the treatment for numerous illnesses.

While these drugs were designed to help cure or treat known illnesses, they soon became the target of unscrupulous people involved in sport who saw performance benefits could be achieved when these substances were supplied to athletes.

At the level of elite sport, the use of the vast majority of these drugs is done through a carefully orchestrated and managed regime which is overseen by either doctors or sports scientists—or, in many circumstances, both.

As a result, there is a certain safety net that protects the athlete when it comes to physical harm.

This approach has come a long way since the days of East Germany, where there appeared to be very few checks and balances as the communist regime of the day saw winning vastly more important than the future health of its athletes.

Nowadays, for example, all professional cycling teams are backed up by significant medical and sports science staff.

History has starkly indicated many of these backroom boys have been the drivers behind the sport being the most tainted in the world when it comes to doping.

But, again, the sports law-breaking doping protocols are undertaken within strict controls both designed to elude the testers and also maintain the health of the cyclist.

But it is only the major teams, with their vast financial backing, that can afford medical support available 24-7 to the riders, whether they be providing their services for either legal or illegal practices in sporting terms.

Once you go below the top tiers of every major elite sport, as expected, the level of direct medical and sports science support rapidly dwindles.

And it is these various strata beneath the elite level that would be impacted the greatest by lifting the bans and sanctions currently in place with respect to doping.

Criteria for Prohibited Substances

For a substance or method to be prohibited, it must meet two of the following three conditions:

1. The substance or method has the potential to enhance, or does enhance performance in sport.

2. The substance or method has the potential to risk the athlete's health.

3. The World Anti-Doping Agency has determined that the substance or method violates the spirit of sport.

Australian Sports Anti-Doping Authority,
"Drugs, Medications, Substances and Methods in Sport,"
Australian Sports Anti-Doping Authority, 2014.
www.asada.gov.au/substances.

When EPO became the drug of choice among the peloton of professional cycling in Europe in the early-1990s it was looked upon as a silver bullet—a drug capable of synthetically enriching the athlete's red blood cell count and, as a result, creating a greater capacity for oxygen transference within the body.

The sports scientists and doctors—many of them unscrupulous in their practice—assisting top tier professional teams were soon clamouring over one another to get their hands on this new wonder drug.

History now indicates in events like the Tour de France the majority of riders were using either EPO or other blood boosting practices to enhance their physiology for much of the era from the mid-1990s onwards.

In the early days of EPO's nexus with cycling there was a spate of deaths—young men who were supremely fit yet nonetheless died in their sleep.

Up to a dozen deaths occurred in a relatively short space of time.

Most of these fatalities were attributed to the use of EPO, which may provide substantial advantages in athletic performance for an endurance athlete while in training or competition but can have a very deleterious effect when the body is at rest, as it can lead to blood thickening, a common cause of heart failure.

Interestingly, almost all the recorded deaths were among cyclists at either amateur level or professionals in teams well down the sport's food chain.

Those particular riders did not have the benefit of readily available medical advice and, as such, most were self-medicating at self-prescribed levels.

By nature, all sportspeople are competitive—they have to be to succeed.

If bans on performance enhancing drugs were lifted across the board and they became a perfectly acceptable part of sport at all levels this inherent competitive streak would likely become a major issue.

If drugs were totally acceptable more athletes would dabble in them—likewise you would expect the same would occur if the laws were lifted with respect to illicit street drugs. The very notion that using the likes of cocaine or heroin is illegal is a major deterrent in itself.

If, for example, two amateur 100m runners are both of similar level and one decides to enhance his performance by using what would have been a previously banned substance, it goes to reason he should eclipse his rival.

If that rival gets wind of his opponent's drug use he may be tempted to go down the same path—and why not, for it is no longer a banned practice in sport?—however having learnt that his rival is on 10mg of a certain drug he decides to use 15mg.

And then, if he starts besting his rival, he may well decide he needs to up his intake and go to 20mg in an endeavour to retain his advantage.

But who is there to advise him on just what levels are safe?

Does he have to pay to go and see a sports physician or does he just think that surely a few more milligrams can't hurt?

Pretty soon things could get very ugly.

Simply throwing our hands in the air and saying to the drug cheats, "you win", is not the solution.

Yes, many may be flaunting the system and slipping through the cracks.

But allowing all sportspeople to go "chemical" with no fear at all of being outed, banned and disgraced is not an acceptable path to follow.

Just like drugs in mainstream society, the battle to eradicate doping in sport is the right thing to do.

Oh, and by the by, sport is actually supposed to produce healthier bodies and minds—simply saying the war on doping is just too difficult is a quick way to potentially torpedo that ethos for good.

Periodical and Internet Sources Bibliography

The following articles have been selected to supplement the diverse views presented in this chapter.

J.C. Bradbury	"Fine the Dirty, Reward the Clean," *New York Times*, August 8, 2012.
Chris Cooper	"Should We Allow Doping in the Tour de France? Or All Sports?" *New Republic*, June 29, 2012.
Margaret Goodman	"Clean Competition Is Safest," *New York Times*, August 8, 2012.
Robert Harding	"Time to Get Tough: Major League Baseball Should Hand Out Lifetime Bans for Doping," Auburnpub.com, July 25, 2013.
Jim Higgins	"Maybe It's Time to Legalize Doping in Pro Sports," VTDigger.com, February 22, 2013.
Nate Jendrick	"In My Mind: Increasing the Doping Ban Is Only a Start," *Swimming World*, December 3, 2012.
Thorn Loverro	"Alex Rodriguez and Lance Armstrong Are Not Heroes—They Are Cheaters," *The Guardian*, August 13, 2013.
Julian Savulescu	"Permit Doping So We Can Monitor It," *New York Times*, August 7, 2012.
Chris Smith	"Why It's Time to Legalize Steroids in Professional Sports," *Forbes*, August 24, 2012.
Ian Steadman	"How Sports Would Be Better with Doping," *Wired*, September 10, 2012.
Steven Wang	"Is It Time to Legalize PEDs?," *The International*, August 10, 2013.

OPPOSING
VIEWPOINTS®
SERIES

CHAPTER 3

What Are the Effects of Doping on Sports?

Chapter Preface

In the early months of 2013, Major League Baseball (MLB) was rocked by new revelations of doping by several well-known baseball players, a sordid affair that became known as the Biogenesis scandal. The *Miami New Times* newspaper published documents from a former employee of Biogenesis, a health clinic in Florida, that linked players Alex Rodriguez, Ryan Braun, and Nelson Cruz to the clinic. All three tested positive for performance-enhancing drugs (PEDs) in 2012, and all three are former patients of the clinic.

The MLB launched an investigation and conducted a series of interviews with players tied to Biogenesis. It also obtained the health records of MLB players who had received treatment from the clinic.

On July 22, 2013, the MLB announced it was suspending Braun for the rest of the baseball season and the play-offs for doping. Although Braun had initially denied that he had ever used PEDs, he did not appeal his suspension. In August Braun released a statement explaining his initial denials and subsequent confession. It read, in part, "During the latter part of the 2011 season, I was dealing with a nagging injury and I turned to products for a short period of time that I shouldn't have used. The products were a cream and a lozenge which I was told could help expedite my rehabilitation. It was a huge mistake for which I am deeply ashamed and I compounded the situation by not admitting my mistakes immediately."

On August 5 the MLB suspended more players, each for fifty games, including Nelson Cruz. That same day, the MLB also announced that it was suspending Alex Rodriguez for 211 games. Rumors had circled for years that Rodriguez had taken PEDs. As a result of its investigation, the MLB found evidence that he had taken various performance-enhancing substances, including testosterone and human growth hormone, over a number of years and had actively attempted to obstruct a MLB investigation into allegations of his doping. Rodriguez immediately appealed his suspension.

MLB commissioner Bud Selig released a statement that accompanied the announcement of the August 5 suspensions that reiterated the league's commitment to antidoping measures. It states, in part, "As a social institution with enormous social responsibilities, Baseball must do everything it can to maintain integrity, fairness, and a level playing field. . . . We are committed to working together with players to reiterate that performance-enhancing drugs will not be tolerated in our game."

This chapter includes viewpoints that examine the different impacts of doping on sports, including its influence on traditional sporting values, fan morale, the level of competition, and on athletes as role models.

> *"For the follower of Christ, sport is not war, and it is not merely fun. It is another context to cultivate and display Christlikeness."*

Doping Destroys Traditional Sports Values

Mike Austin

In the following viewpoint, written in October 2012, Mike Austin identifies two contemporary views of sports that he says are morally problematic and should be rejected by moral and spiritual people. One view is that sport is a type of war, a perspective that, according to Austin, can lead to ruthlessness and moral dissolution, including the use of performance-enhancing drugs (PEDs). The other view is that sport is merely for fun, which Austin says ignores key aspects of competition, such as integrity, courage, and perseverance. Austin concludes that using PEDs is counter to Christian values, because it is self-centered, unethical, and weak. Mike Austin is an author, blogger, and professor of philosophy at Eastern Kentucky University.

As you read, consider the following questions:

1. According to Mike Austin, what was Lance Armstrong's highest finish in the Tour de France now that he has been stripped of all seven of his titles?

2. What 1981 movie does Austin reference to make a point about the relationship between religion and sport?

3. What did Joey Cheek say about humility in sport, according to Austin?

In recent weeks, the doping scandal surrounding [American cyclist] Lance Armstrong has taken center stage, bringing a troubling aspect of the sport of cycling back into the limelight. Armstrong has been officially stripped of all seven of his Tour de France titles. This means that his highest finish at the Tour de France is now 36th, his place in the 1995 race. And Greg LeMond is once again the only American to win this prestigious event. While Armstrong's case provides food for thought related to many important issues, here I will focus on a Christian perspective concerning the nature and value of sport and some of its implications for the ethics of performance-enhancing drugs.

Sport and Spirituality

For the follower of Christ, sport will be a context in which one can express love for God as well as a concern for His glory. In one of the most memorable scenes from the 1981 film *Chariots of Fire*, aspiring Olympian Eric Liddell and his sister Jennie discuss his plans to compete in the 1924 Olympics. She expresses her reticence about this; she is worried that success on the track might derail his plans to be a missionary in China. Jennie is momentarily relieved to hear him confirm that he plans to go to China. However, she is taken aback when he adds:

> But I've got a lot of running to do first. Jennie, Jennie, you've got to understand. I believe that God made me for a purpose, for China. But He also made me fast. And when I run, I feel His pleasure. To give it up would be to hold Him in contempt. You were right, it's not just fun. To win is to honor Him.

Greg Lemond

In May of 1983, [American cyclist Greg] LeMond's third professional season, he took first place in the Dauphiné Libéré stage race, and then followed with a fourth-place finish in the Tour of Switzerland. His greatest victory to date came, however, at the 1983 World Road Race Championship, becoming the first cyclist from the United States to win this race. In recognition of his 1983 accomplishments, LeMond was awarded the Super Prestige Pernod Trophy, marking him as the best cyclist of the year.

In 1984, LeMond's fourth year as a professional cyclist, he made his debut in the world's most prestigious and difficult race, the Tour de France. Although he got off to a shaky start in the 23-day, 2,500-mile race, he finished third, becoming the first non-European to mount the winner's podium.

Bernard Hinault, LeMond's teammate of 1983, had spent the 1984 season racing for a new team, the French-based La Vie Claire. As the 1985 season approached, Hinault asked LeMond if he would join La Vie Claire and ride as cocaptain. LeMond accepted the offer, and in the Tour de France of that year put his personal ambitions aside and helped Hinault to win his fifth Tour while LeMond took second place. The 1986 edition of the Tour de France began with the expectation that LeMond would be the favorite to win, seconded by Hinault, the defending champion. It soon became clear that this was not entirely the case. Rather than working with LeMond, Hinault "attacked" his teammate again and again. It was only through immense force of will in the face of an apparent betrayal and a partisan French crowd that LeMond took the overall victory.

"Greg Lemond," Biography in Context Online Collection. *Detroit, MI: Gale, 2013.*

It is clear that it is not mere victory that Liddell is after, but an honorable victory that is the fruit of spiritual, moral, and physical excellence—with a bit of fun added into the mix as well.

Two contemporary views of sport are distinct from Liddell's. They are in fact morally problematic and should be rejected by those who want to think Christianly about sport. For instance, when sport is viewed as war, this can lead to treating opponents as enemies and a failure to respect them as persons. The "sport as war" view can also lead to a win-at-all-costs attitude which may foster the use of performance-enhancing drugs, other forms of cheating (such as diving in soccer), and the cultivation of vice. Another prominent view, which takes sport to be mere play, is also morally suspect. For instance, we often tell children that sports are "just for fun," but from a Christian perspective this is misguided. Participation in sport *merely* for fun can lead to a self-centered and consumer-approach to sport. Sports are certainly fun, but they are more than that; they also provide a context for displaying and cultivating character. For the follower of Christ, sport is not war, and it is not merely fun. It is another context to cultivate and display Christlikeness.

Sport as Character Development

Consider one example of character-development via sport. Though it is rare, perhaps, humility is an important sporting virtue. Sport can foster humility in both athletes and coaches, who must submit themselves to the standards of their sport if they wish to excel or (even just participate) in it. These standards not only include the formal rules, but the informal ones as well. Humility can also be acquired via sport as an athlete reflects on the numerous causes of his success. While it is true that an athlete is responsible in part for success at the elite level, given all the work and dedication that this requires, the reflective athlete will also see that there is reason to be humble even in the midst of great success. As 2006 Olympic gold medalist [American] speed skater Joey Cheek puts it, "a lot of people . . . don't realize the sheer dumb luck that goes into being born into a country and a family that has the means and resources to allow you to chase your dreams." The Christian will likely substitute God's providence for luck here, but the point remains that humility is an appropriate attitude to take, even for the most successful athlete. And of course many other virtues can be cultivated via sport, including self-control, perseverance, and certain forms of courage.

The use of performance-enhancing drugs undermines a character-focused approach to sport. Competition at its best is a test of athletic ability and other forms of excellence. But as philosopher of sport Robert Simon argues in his book *Fair Play: The Ethics of Sport*, when drugs are the cause of improved play on the field or a faster time on the roads, the winner ends up being the person whose body responds best to some performance-enhancing drug, rather than the best athlete who delivers the best performance on a given day. The athlete who is concerned about her character prefers depending on virtues such as courage, discipline, and perseverance in her quest for victory, rather than drugs. She wants the cause of her athletic success to be of the right sort. Disciplined training, responding to coaching, and proper nutrition call upon the virtues, but using performance-enhancing drugs does not.

The temptations of fame and fortune loom large in much of contemporary sport, as does the win-at-all-costs attitude. All of this may motivate one to use performance-enhancing drugs. These negative aspects of the contemporary scene shouldn't lead us to reject sport. Rather, they underscore the need to keep sport in its proper place, as a form of competitive play that is a partial foretaste of life in the kingdom of God. Sport can be spiritually dangerous—as can many other worthwhile endeavors—but it can also provide a context for cultivating and exemplifying spiritual, moral, intellectual, and physical virtue. The crucial point for the Christian is that sport should serve as a way, in the words of Eric Liddell, "to honor Him."

"Sports are awash in drugs. Why would professional basketball be any different?"

Doping Provides an Unfair Advantage

Patrick Hruby

In the following viewpoint, Patrick Hruby contends that the National Basketball Association (NBA) has a doping problem similar to many other sports, including baseball, cycling, and track. He maintains that basketball players reap the same benefits from PEDs as athletes in other sports. Hruby argues that PEDs help muscles recuperate from physical exercise, letting basketball players train longer and perform at a high level for a longer period of time; accelerate healing and muscle tissue repair; and boost endurance by bringing more oxygen to muscles and speeding up removal of metabolic waste. Hruby concludes that basketball does not drug test its athletes as much as other sports, and if it did, many players would fail the tests. Patrick Hruby is a sportswriter for the website Sports on Earth.

As you read, consider the following questions:

1. According to Patrick Hruby, what Orlando Magic player was suspended for twenty games by the NBA in February 2013 after testing positive for steroids?

2. What Memphis Grizzlies guard does Hruby report was issued a ten-game suspension by the NBA for a failed drug test?

3. How many positive drugs tests for US athletes were covered up by the United States Olympic Committee from 1988 to 2000, according to Hruby?

Maybe you missed it. Probably you missed it. Earlier this week, Orlando Magic forward Hedo Turkoglu was suspended 20 games by the NBA after testing positive for steroids.

Here's what didn't happen next.

Demands for more stringent drug testing. Calls for Congressional hearings. Comparisons to [American cyclist] Lance Armstrong. I-told-you-so tweets from [American baseball player] José Canseco. Wailing over Turkoglu's career statistics. Gnashing of teeth over his place in basketball history. Concern that this sets a bad example for the children. Concern that this sets a bad example for *other dopers*. (Seriously: Turkoglu took a left on Anabolic Avenue, and all he has to show for it 2.9 points and 2.4 rebounds per game? Did his methenolone [an anabolic steroid] get mixed up with a bag of oregano?)

Turkoglu's swift mea culpa and dubious-sounding excuse—he took mystery medication from a trainer in Turkey last summer to recover from a shoulder injury, and whaddya know, he forgot to check it against the league's list of banned substances—was not met with . . . pronounced public snickering. . . . Federal agents did not pick through Turkoglu's trash. Anti-doping officials did not appear on [the television program] *60 Minutes* to press for a detailed confession. No one connected the potential dots between Turkoglu and former Magic teammate Rashard Lewis, who also flunked a steroid screen in 2009; no one, *not even on the Internet,* took the next conspiracy-minded step and wondered how, exactly, former Magic frontcourt mate Dwight Howard's bulbous shoulders became bigger than [American baseball player] Barry Bonds' head.

To the contrary, nobody cared. Not really. Nobody cared because the NBA got the same pass it always gets, because everybody knows that professional basketball—a ferociously competitive, highly lucrative sport that puts a premium on running, jumping, strength and endurance, not to mention rapid recovery during a long, physically taxing season—does not have a performance-enhancing drug problem.

Right?

Doping in the NBA

David Stern seems to think so. In 2005, the league commissioner said that PED use wasn't "a problem at the present time that we think we have." [Retired NBA player] Charles Barkley seems to think so, too: four years ago, he expressed surprise at Lewis' steroid suspension, arguing that tall, lithe NBA players simply don't have physiques that suggest widespread doping. Around the same time Stern made his comment, a longtime NBA athletic trainer told ESPN.com's Marc Stein that "in the basketball culture, players want to be long and athletic. They want to be lean, and they would be fearful that added bulk would affect their lateral quickness;" a team physician said that "when you're playing every other night for 82 games, endurance is really what you're after, and steroids actually hurt that;" and 15-year league veteran Tony Massenburg added that NBA players don't even *like* to lift weights.

Of course, all of this makes perfect sense. Provided you have no idea how PEDs can actually enhance, you know, performance.

"That makes *no* sense," says former Bay Area Laboratory Co-Operative (BALCO) mastermind Victor Conte. "Look at the biceps of Tour de France riders. They're 9–10 inches [in circumference]. We know they use anabolic steroids, specifically testosterone. For the most part, these drugs—meaning the whole category of anabolic steroids—are recovery drugs. They are very powerful. Would they be a benefit to an NBA player? Absolutely."

Charles Yesalis, a Penn State emeritus professor and sports doping expert, concurs.

"Distance runners have been using anabolics and growth hormones in very small doses for years," he says. "Not to build muscle. But to help recuperate. The myth of [PEDs] making you muscle-bound is so over."

A Logical Conclusion

I believe NBA players are using steroids. Human growth hormone. Stimulants like Adderall. The blood-boosting drug erythropoietin (EPO). Anything and everything to get an edge. I believe players are doping in the summer and doping in season and doping during All-Star Weekend, stacking and microdosing, injecting and rubbing in cream. Do I have smoking-gun proof? Nothing beyond the occasional failed drug test, like the one that earned then-Memphis Grizzlies guard O.J. Mayo a 10-game suspension in 2011. Is use widespread, like Chicago Bulls guard Derrick Rose reportedly once suggested and then denied? I have no idea.

Still, I'm convinced it's happening. So is Yesalis, who after Lewis' suspension told me there was "no doubt in his mind." To think otherwise is to have both admirable faith in the better angels of human nature and a willful disregard for basic logic. "The money involved is substantial," Yesalis says. "The drugs are available. The tests are fraught with loopholes. I don't know how complicated it is. It's the same as all other sports. Why would anybody think the NBA is any cleaner than baseball?" To think otherwise is to sound like Stern, who in 2005 delivered the following prepared statement to a Congressional committee, and only walked away a free man because declaring one's studious belief in the existence of Bigfoot before a group of skeptical lawmakers is not, in fact, a federal crime:

> The sport of basketball emphasizes a specialized set of physical abilities—particularly quickness, agility and basketball skill—that are distinct from those required in a number of other sports. Accordingly, illicit substances that could assist athletes in strength sports [such as weightlifting and football], power sports [such as baseball], or endurance sports [such as cycling or marathon running], are not likely to be of benefit to NBA players.

Ahem. Conte tells a story. Back when he was helping athletes dope, he gave EPO to one of his female sprinters. (Conte declines to provide her name, but it's easy to infer he's talking about retired sprinter Kelli White.) White won two gold medals at the 2003 world championships. When she subsequently confessed to PED use during the height of the BALCO scandal [a federal investigation initiated in 2002 found Bay Area Laboratory Co-operative (BALCO), a company that offered blood and urine testing, to be providing athletes with PEDs], anti-doping scientists such as Don Catlin found one part of her drug cocktail baffling: *why was a sprinter taking EPO, a drug that boosts endurance by increasing the blood's oxygen-carrying capacity?*

"What they failed to ask was this: how long do you think these athletes train each day?" Conte says. "Hours and hours. And in the offseason, training for months and months, do you think that a deeper training load wouldn't help you? These are training drugs!"

EPO Effects

When Conte first began studying the physiology of athletic performance, he says, he was particularly intrigued by Defense Department research on Navy SEALs, whose bodies and minds are subjected to extreme levels of strain and stress during intense training exercises. "They go through hand-to-hand combat, verbal abuse, sleep deprivation, underwater demolition," he says. "It depletes the body of nutrients and builds up metabolic waste products. I saw parallels with elite athletes."

Growth hormone, Conte says, could help NBA players maintain muscle mass over the course of a long, punishing season. Anabolic steroids accelerate muscle tissue repair and healing, which could help with recovery from both hard training and hard-luck injury. EPO boosts endurance not only by bringing more oxygen to muscles, but also by speeding up removal of metabolic waste, delaying the onset of fatigue.

"I have heard a lot of athletes in the NFL [National Football League] and track and field describe the effect of EPO with one word," he says. "It makes you like a *machine*. You just don't get tired. In basketball, you might not see the effect as much in the first and second quarter, but by the fourth quarter there's a huge edge. One guy has a body full of toxins that have built up. The other guy has a body that has accelerated the removal of those toxins. He's the one who will be able to make that quick move and get past his defender."

Chasing Career Longevity

In baseball, widespread use of PEDs inverted the usual relationship between advancing age and declining production: 30-something players were suddenly becoming better as they got older. In the NBA, a group of aging stars including Los Angeles Lakers guards Kobe Bryant and Steve Nash spent much of the last half-decade managing to pull off a similar trick; was it, as [the website] Grantland's [editor-in-chief] Bill Simmons has argued, the result of "better doctors, surgical procedures, dieting, drug testing, trainers, computers, video equipment, workout equipment, workout regiments, airplanes" and even "hotel pillows?" Or was something else afoot?

Remember: during MLB's [Major League Baseball's] 1990s size-and-power surge, before BALCO and the Mitchell Report [a 2007 report on an investigation of PED use in the MLB], people were writing straight-faced articles about [professional baseball player] Ken Caminiti's "goody bag"—full of all-natural vitamins and nutritional supplements—and how creatine and weight training alone were changing the sport.

"The level of these hormones like growth hormone and testosterone begin to decline in the body on average at age 30," Conte says. "At least a one percent drop per year. So guys getting up in their 30s are not going to recover like they would be in their mid 20s. That's another way [PEDs] can help."

Inadaquate Drug Testing Policy

If NBA players have ample incentives to use PEDs—millions of guaranteed dollars at stake; the not-insubstantial fact that the drugs *work*—they also have few disincentives. After all, federal lawmakers labeled the league's drug testing policy "inadequate," "pathetic" and "a joke" in 2005, and again blasted the NBA three years later. Last October [2012], World Anti-Doping Agency director general David Howman said the league had "gaps" in its program—gaps that ESPN.com [sportswriter] Henry Abbott identified as:

- A lack of blood testing, which means the league cannot detect HGH [human growth hormone] use;

- A lack of "biological passports," a year-round assessment of an athlete's blood profile that looks for chemical oddities and has been credited with reducing doping in cycling;

- A vulnerability to micro-dosing, a practice in which athletes take small doses of PEDs that clear the body in a matter of hours, giving testers a tiny window of opportunity;

- Advance notice to players of drug tests, particularly in the off-season, which gives players time to prepare and/or make themselves scarce.

Abbott also points out that the NBA only subjects players to four random tests per season and just two random tests in the off-season. Both numbers make Conte incredulous. "Testing you only a couple of times a year isn't much, especially when you know how quickly some of these drugs clear," he says. "EPO, synthetic testosterone, you can clear them in a day. And the off-season is when the fish are really biting. If you don't put your hook and line in the pond when you know they're biting, you're not going to catch any fish. I believe that there are really all sorts of loopholes in the testing of the NBA."

A Gut Instinct

Yesalis trusts his eyes. Are NBA players as muscular as their NFL counterparts? No. But they're bigger, faster and stronger than their predecessors. More defined, too. "Just get a bunch of pictures of pro basketball players in the 1960s and 1970s," he says. "Look at how they've changed." In the early 1980s, Yesalis was a college strength coach. He remembers women's basketball players at major conference programs lifting weights. "Basketball players have been lifting for more than 30 years," he says. "The notion that they're bigger and stronger just because they started lifting weights is a bunch of crap. That can't explain it. You can't use that as an excuse."

Maybe Yesalis is wrong. Conte, too. Maybe I'm wrong. I'd like to be. I'd like to believe Turkoglu is a sad, bizarre outlier, that the reason only eight NBA players since 2000 have been caught and suspended for PED use is that *NBA players don't use PEDs.* Thing is, history suggests otherwise. Americans once scoffed at East Germany's no-good, very-bad, lyin' and cheatin' glow-in-the-dark Olympic athletes—that is, until we learned that the United States Olympic Committee may have covered up more than 100 positive drugs tests for U.S. athletes who won 19 Olympics medals from 1988–2000. . . . In her 2004 autobiography, [American sprinter] Marion Jones covered an entire page in large red letters reading: *I AM AGAINST PERFORMANCE ENHANCING DRUGS. I HAVE NEVER TAKEN THEM AND I NEVER WILL TAKE THEM.* Armstrong told his doubters that he was "sorry you don't believe in miracles." When the Carolina Panthers were caught up in a Super Bowl steroids scandal, not even their punter was immune. Years after his good boy sweater-wearing doping confession, [American baseball player] Alex Rodriguez is allegedly still hanging out with Cousin Yuri [Rodriguez's cousin, Yuri Sucart, allegedly provided the player with PEDs]. So it goes. Sports are awash in drugs. Why would professional basketball be any different? "It's the same story with all of these sports," Conte says. "If you have the financial incentive and the inept testing, and you are part of a culture where you believe your opponents are using drugs, you do what you have to do in order to be competitive. I'm not as familiar with NBA culture, but I know that all the same elements are there."

In 2004, Conte appeared on ABC's *20/20* [television show], giving an interview in which he fingered Jones and insisted that the Olympics were rife with PEDs, corruption and cover-ups. Many scoffed. Almost a decade later, he's gone from pariah to prophet, and his disquieting message—the one that very well may apply to the same NBA that has built an entire unironic marketing campaign around the word *big*—hasn't changed.

"There is no Santa Claus, Easter Bunny or Tooth Fairy," he says. "Not at the elite level of sport."

"Whether we want to believe it or not, it is impacting our youth and their attitudes about what one must do to compete at the higher levels."

Athletes Who Use Performance-Enhancing Drugs Are Not Good Role Models

Kirk Mango

In the following viewpoint, Kirk Mango asserts that allowing performance-enhancing drugs (PEDs) in sports would have a negative impact on youth. He argues that if kids start to believe that doping is a normal and acceptable part of being an elite athlete, it directly contradicts efforts to promote ethics and character development in youth sports. Mango concludes that sports are a microcosm of society, and it is imperative that adults teach the right lessons to kids by not sending the message that doping is acceptable. Kirk Mango is a journalist, blogger, and the author of the book, Becoming a True Champion: Achieving Athletic Excellence from the Inside Out.

Kirk Mango, "Big Deal!!! Lance Armstrong Used PEDs? So What?," *Chicago Now*, 2013. www.becomingatruechampion.com. Kirk Mango is the author of *Becoming a True Champion*, a former National Champion, three-time All-American, three-time Hall of Fame athlete, and veteran educator. Reproduced by permission.

As you read, consider the following questions:

1. According to Kirk Mango, on what television show did Lance Armstrong admit to doping?

2. What sports talk radio host does Mango say came out strongly against the doping culture?

3. Who is the board director and vice president of the Center for Ethical Youth Coaching, according to Mango?

There are those who believe that too much has been made of [American cyclist] Lance Armstrong's use of PED's [performance-enhancing drugs], that his recent admission on Oprah [television show *Oprah's Next Chapter*, hosted by Oprah Winfrey] was pointless, that his work with cancer through his Livestrong Foundation should supersede *all* as it has helped so many. There are also those (likely a good number from the same group above) who think since so many [other cyclists] were using when Lance was competing that his use didn't matter, that it was a supposed "even" playing field, and that so many are using in so many sports that PED use should be allowed and just regulated.

Me ... I'm *NOT* one of those aforementioned. I am nowhere near in that thinking as I fall completely on the opposite end of the scale, and I am not alone.

The Consequences of a Doping Culture

Take [radio sports commentator] Mike Golic's comments (Mike & Mike on ESPN Radio out of Chicago) on [his cohost radio sports commentator] Mike Greenberg questioning whether it is time to allow PED's in sports and just regulate them as it seems obvious their use has become rampant. . . .

Golic emphasizes that allowing and regulating performance-enhancement drugs in sports would make the problem much worse . . . not better. That it would have a larger, more global impact . . . especially with our youth. . . .

Golic's observations ... are so crystal clear that they resonate strongly with me, as I also believe what he said to be accurate. Mike ... hat's off to you, your remarks are right on point.

Continuing this discussion, and bringing it back to Lance Armstrong, take the Center for Ethical Youth Coaching's (CEYC) position on all this. And let me reemphasize here that word *ETHICAL* in their title as it is an important piece to this whole issue of PED use. You see ... there is much more at stake than little old Lance and his "bad," unethical, self-serving behavior.

The New Normal

It is something many negate, or simply don't see, as they accept what he did as a normal part of being an elite level athlete, something they believe society has no right to meddle in as it is his right as an individual to choose to use or not, and something that really has no important impact on anyone else other than him and cycling.

I suppose if we look at this situation with a very narrow focus, basically with blinders on (those things horses wear to keep their vision forward), or we view Lance's "cheating" in light of the awful tragedy of Sandy Hook [elementary school where a gunman shot and killed twenty-six children and staff in 2012] (or despicable Penn State scandal and Jerry Sandusky [former Penn State football coach who was convicted of child molestation in 2012]), I can certainly see that point.

However, as is true with many things, even though the lies Armstrong vehemently told for many years (then turn a big 180 well after so much evidence became public) don't come close to the two terrible and shocking circumstances previously mentioned ... it still is well beyond the "middle" of the scale. And whether one wants to "see" it or not ... it does have negative impact on our youth, and, from my perspective, with society as a whole.

Paul Fell/www.CartoonStock.com.

The Impact on Youth

And that's where the Center for Ethical Youth Coaching enters the picture. In a recent news release, board director and vice president, Dr. John Mayer (clinical psychology from Northwestern University Medical School), clarifies the impact Lance's behavior has had on youth.

> I am in schools every day and I have been polling students on their reaction to the anticipated Armstrong revelation on the Oprah Show. The reaction is divided between, "Oh well, another great athlete has cheated to get glory." and, "He was one (athlete) we could believe in." and, "No surprise, they all cheat to win."

> The harm this does to young people hungry for role models is devastating.

The fall of Lance Armstrong as a role model for young athletes is a huge hit to our efforts to promote ethics and character development in youth sports.

Armstrong was so adamant about his innocence, kids looked at him as one of the good guys who was doing it right and engaging in ethical participation.

So what does that say to our youth about high level sports competition and the athletes who compete at that level? The answer is obvious.

Whether we want to believe it or not, it is impacting our youth and their attitudes about what one must do to compete at the higher levels. Kids *are* growing up in a culture that believes this is the way it is for all, that this is *how* someone gets really good, that it is just a *normal* part of being an athlete. To me, that's about one step away from becoming, well . . . acceptable—OK!!!

And when we look at society as a whole . . . aren't we seeing similar attitudes? That it is normal . . . OK, to cheat, to do *whatever* it takes no matter the consequence to anyone, to "win" through making more money, gaining more power, even getting better grades, regardless of how one might go about gaining those things—a "win at all costs" attitude.

A Cheating Culture

Couldn't we say that our sports culture these days, Armstrong being only one example, is simply reflecting a culture that is moving toward a thought process that says "cheating . . . doing whatever I need to, to get what I want, is just fine as long as I don't get caught"?

(And it might come as a surprise to some that, as a veteran educator, I have heard students say these exact words about cheating, "if you don't get caught, you've done nothing wrong.")

Couldn't we say that what we are seeing in sports today is simply a microcosm of society as a whole, more loudly reflecting the same attitudes and beliefs?

So yes, there are worse things than the Lance Armstrong doping scandal, but ... to dismiss it as an unimportant issue that has little impact on anyone other than Lance Armstrong and/or cycling is an error society cannot afford.

"By telling them it's ok to worship these men and women, we are teaching them to support everything that is wrong with the world."

Athletes Should Not Be Regarded As Role Models

Rochelle Ballin

In the following viewpoint, Rochelle Ballin contends that it is time to stop allowing athletes to be role models to children. She views professional cyclist Lance Armstrong, who admitted to doping and was stripped of his Tour de France titles, as just the latest in a long line of athletes who have lied, cheated, and betrayed the public. Ballin concludes that children should be encouraged to look up to people who make the world a better place, such as teachers. Rochelle Ballin is a contributor to the website Title to Be Determined.

As you read, consider the following questions:

1. What three baseball players does Rochelle Ballin name from the steroid era?

2. Does Ballin believe that any of the baseball players from the steroid era will eventually be voted into the National Baseball Hall of Fame and Museum?

> 3. What does Ballin think will happen to Lance Armstrong?

Now that Lance Armstrong has admitted to doping, deceiving and destroying lives, can we stop allowing athletes to be major role models for our children? He isn't the only doping athlete, he is just the most recent in a long line of "great" athletes that are supposed to be the best of the best.

Armstrong spent the last thirteen years [since 1999] covering up one lie after another and lashing out on anyone who dared to tell the truth about him. This is not the kind of person children should look to for guidance on how to live.

An Illusion

Along with the Steroid Era [period from the late 1980s through the late 2000s during which many professional baseball players used steroids] baseball players—Mark McGwire, Sammy Sosa and Roger Clemens, to name a few—Armstrong has let people down. He created an empire based on an image of perseverance, truth and the power of self-preservation. He was what we would like children to grow up to be. Unfortunately, the image he created is just an illusion. An illusion that fooled millions of people, especially every person who ever bought a Livestrong bracelet and gave to his [cancer] charity [the Lance Armstrong Foundation, renamed in 2012 as the Livestrong Foundation].

Like people are turning against him out of anger or confusion, but it's disappointment. No one asked Armstrong to be great. No one made him take steroids or forced him back on a bike after he completed his chemotherapy [Armstrong was diagnosed with testicular cancer in 1996]. He made those choices on his own. He put himself in a position to gain fame and notoriety. He wanted to be glorified and he was. He made cycling popular in this country [the United States]. He became the spokesperson of an entire sport. Ask your Average Joe on

Sammy Sosa

In 1998, Sammy Sosa became the second baseball player that year to break Roger Maris's 1961 record of 61 home runs in a season. The Chicago Cubs outfielder [Sosa] ran neck and neck throughout the year with St. Louis Cardinals first baseman Mark McGwire as enthusiastic fans watched to see who would hit 62 first. Though McGwire did so on September 8, Sosa soon followed on his heels, slugging his not even a week later. Many credited the friendly race to see who would surpass the mark that had stood for 37 years with invigorating baseball. Although some critics noted that McGwire got a lot more attention in the press than Sosa, the latter never seemed to mind sharing the spotlight. However, Sosa's achievements were later marred by his use of a corked bat and by allegations that he used performance-enhancing steroids.

"Sammy Sosa," Biography in Context Online Collection.
Detroit, MI: Gale, 2009.

the street to name another cyclist and you'd be hard pressed to find someone who can name a cyclist beyond Armstrong.

Athletes as Role Models

Now that he has been exposed and admitted to his crimes, we have to explain, yet again, to children what has happened to yet another hero. The problem, aside from explaining that sometimes people will do things that disappoint you, is that he shouldn't have been their role model in the first place. Neither should have Roger Clemens or Mark McGwire or Sammy Sosa. They do not save the world. They do not sacrifice their lives in order to make the world a better place. They play a game, run a race. What they do isn't important in the grand scheme of the world.

Instead children should look up to a doctor who volunteers his time, a teacher who spends time after school tutoring students or even a parent who works two jobs to keep clothes on their back and a roof over their heads. We are living in a world now where we are teaching children that those things don't really matter as long as you can hit a ball and jump really high or run really fast. We are living in a world that teaches them if they can't do those things, take drugs to help you and when you get caught make sure you point as many fingers as possible. If their ship is going down, take as many people down with you as possible.

End the Cycle

We are teaching our children to lie, cheat, steal and distrust. By telling them it's ok to worship these men and women, we are teaching them to support everything that is wrong with the world. Although the journalists voting for the baseball hall of fame [the National Baseball Hall of Fame and Museum in Cooperstown, New York] this year [2013] were deadlocked and chose no one, eventually one of the Steroid Era players, if not all, will make it to Cooperstown [be inducted into the hall of fame]. Lance Armstrong will eventually fade into oblivion. Other stellar physical specimens will emerge and we will allow ourselves to forget what happened in the past. We will allow ourselves to become so enamored with the game and athletic prowess again that we will be duped again. We will allow ourselves to be outraged again. We will have to explain to a new generation of children that people will disappoint them.

Nobody is perfect. No one should expect anyone to be, but we do anyway. We do only to have to deal with the agony of betrayal. There are so many other things in the world that will disappoint and betray us, why let this be one of them? Why give athletes the power to let us down like this? We have to stop allowing them this power. The cycle will never end if we don't. And maybe if we stop expecting the perfection, athletes will stop feeling the pressure and tainting sports will be history. That may be wishful thinking, but a girl can dream, can't she?

> *"In light of what everyone now knows about the depths of depravity during the EPO [erythropoietin] era, can any reasonable observer honestly believe that today's stars are racing and winning clean?"*

Analysis: Nibali's Giro Win Represents Quandary of "New" Cycling

Andrew Hood

In the following viewpoint, written in May 2013, Andrew Hood examines the cloud of suspicion hovering over Italian cyclist Vincenzo Nibali's 2013 victory at the Giro d'Italia, one of the sport's biggest races. Hood contends that in light of various doping scandals, it is not unreasonable to suspect that any cyclist who executes a superlative physical performance may be doping. Hood concludes that it may be time to give cyclists like Nibali the benefit of the doubt and applaud their wins as terrific competitive performances. Andrew Hood is a journalist and the European correspondent for the website Velo News.

Andrew Hood, "Nibali's Giro Win Represents Quandary of 'New' Cycling," *Velo News*. Reprinted with permission. The original story, written by Andrew Hood, appeared on VeloNews.com on May 30, 2013.

As you read, consider the following questions:

1. According to Andrew Hood, how many substances are on the banned list of the World Anti-Doping Code?

2. How many times has Danilo Di Luca tested positive for banned substances since 2009, according to Hood?

3. How long was Riccardo Riccò banned for doping, according to Hood?

Vincenzo Nibali (Astana) made his pursuit of pink look easy en route to winning the 96th Giro d'Italia on Sunday. But it is that ease that has many observers questioning the methods the 28-year-old Sicilian used to land his second grand tour title in superb fashion.

Nibali rode an impeccable Giro from start to finish. The "Shark of Messina" barely made a mistake during a weather-marred corsa rosa, and confirmed himself as Italy's newest grand tour champion. But just as Bradley Wiggins (Sky) discovered last year after winning the Tour de France in equally impeccable fashion, victory in today's scandal-weary peloton brings inevitable doubts. Following Nibali's smooth domination of the Giro, can and should we believe his victory was clean?

In light of what everyone now knows about the depths of depravity during the EPO era, can any reasonable observer honestly believe that today's stars are racing and winning clean?

Those are fair questions to ask.

Skeptics see plenty in Nibali's performance over three weeks to raise some eyebrows.

First off, Nibali seemed immune to the cold, suffering, and otherwise miserable conditions that the rest of the peloton endured during the Giro's worst weather in two decades. The Italian, who has one of the best poker faces in the peloton, appeared to be breathing through a straw while others rode with mouths agape through the three-week test of survival. Other than crashing on a wet descent—while attacking—in the first week, Nibali never had a bad moment.

Second, there are serious questions about the legacy of the Astana team and some of its key members. The team's general manager is none other than Alexander Vinokourov, who served a two-year ban for blood doping and was one of the biggest stars during the darkest days of the EPO era in the 1990s and 2000s. Giuseppi Martinelli, Astana's veteran sport director, led the likes of Marco Pantani and Stefano Garzelli to Giro victories. Pantani was ousted from the 1999 Giro while wearing the pink jersey due to high hematocrit levels; Garzelli served a suspension stemming from a positive control for the banned diuretic probenecid at the 2002 Giro. In light of what was revealed by the U.S. Anti-Doping Agency's investigation into the U.S. Postal Service team and other anti-doping inquiries, it's not a stretch to place suspicion on anyone with major success in the EPO era—particularly those with grand tour wins on their palmares.

And the overriding suspicion remains that no one can race, survive, attack, and then win a three-week, 3,000-kilometer grand tour without pharmaceutical assistance. Doping was such an ingrained part of the culture of being a professional cyclist that it seems like an impossible leap of logic to accept that suddenly the peloton is racing on pane y acqua.

Danilo Di Luca's positive control for EPO—announced during the race but tied to an out-of-competition test in late April—reconfirmed that doping remains part of the fabric of the peloton. (Officials are still waiting for results of Di Luca's B sample.) Yet the Di Luca scandal also reveals just how much things have changed between 2007, when "the Killer" won the Giro, and Nibali's victory last week.

A Long Way from Di Luca to Nibali

Di Luca's win in 2007 and Nibali's in 2013 are worlds apart.

First, the noose around the doper's neck is tighter than ever before. Back in the 1990s, there wasn't even a test to detect EPO, and doping controls were notoriously loose and inadequate. Since then, there has been a sea change that has made for very dangerous waters for dopers.

In the wake of the Festina Affaire in 1998, the World Anti-Doping Agency and the World Anti-Doping Code have been enacted. The Code includes more than 1,000 substances on its banned list. A new battery of tests has been developed to detect a wide menu of banned chemical concoctions.

Detection levels have also increased dramatically. Alberto Contador was busted for clenbuterol in 2010 with levels so minute—50 picograms—that only one lab in the world could detect it.

Another loophole that dopers used to exploit was the question of out-of-competition testing. Until a decade ago, tests were only conducted during races. Drugs such as EPO and testosterone take days, weeks, and sometimes months of application to take full effect, but would quickly wash out of the system, meaning that riders rarely doped with easily detectable products during actual competition. They did most of the heavy dosages before a race. Today's pros, under the ADAMs whereabouts program, can be tested anywhere at any time, and must be available to testers 365 days a year.

Several nations have enacted tough anti-doping laws, which give police and investigators sweeping powers for going after doping rings. Armstrong and his doping empire didn't ultimately crumble until witnesses faced potential jail time for perjury if they lied under grand jury testimony. While the USADA case was ultimately built on cooperative witness testimony in exchange for lesser bans, Armstrong would have never fallen had it not been for increased judicial pressure and oversight.

Perhaps most important, the biological passport, introduced in 2006, provides an X-ray of sorts inside the body of athletes, allowing anti-doping officials (and teams) to see what their riders are up to. When applied properly, the passport can be used directly to hand down bans, or even more effectively, provide a baseline to initiate target testing. Riders with suspicious numbers are barraged with tests, and they invariably get popped if they're up to something.

Despite evidence that the anti-doping effort has been bungled, under-funded, and mismanaged, the overall system has gone a long way toward making it harder and harder for dopers to get away with it. The most blatant cheaters are getting caught, something that represents a quantum leap from less than a decade ago. Just ask Di Luca; he's been busted twice now since 2009.

At the same time as these changes on the legal and medical front, there has been a quiet yet equally dramatic transformation from within the peloton.

If you believe what riders say on and off the record, there is evidence that doping has become a minority within the peloton. Teams, managers, and riders have, for a variety of reasons, simply stopped institutionalized doping.

Young riders coming into the sport over the past few years insist they have never seen a needle, been offered a pill or a bag of blood, nor heard of teammates or bosses talking about doping. And those same riders are winning important races, so to them, the proof's in the pudding. If the peloton wasn't cleaning up, the logic goes, they wouldn't be even close to winning anything.

In that context, we come back to the pink jersey question: can and should we believe Nibali?

Can and Should We Believe Nibali?

Nibali has been discreet throughout his career and turned pro just as the seeds of change started to take root. He has never been linked to a major doping scandal nor failed a doping control.

The biggest stink occurred in 2009, when reports surfaced in the Italian media that Ivano Fanini, manager at Amore e

Vita, claimed that sources told him that Nibali was training with the infamous Dr. Michele Ferrari near St. Moritz, Switzerland. Those reports created a firestorm in Italy. Nibali vehemently denied having ever met Ferrari, and threatened to sue Fanini and certain Italian media outlets.

During this Giro, Nibali was indeed in a "class of his own," as Cadel Evans (BMC Racing) put it best, but against whom? Nibali was head and shoulders above a field full of aging stars and young up-and-comers that came into the Giro without realistic hopes of winning.

The peloton's top grand tour riders—Chris Froome (Sky), Contador (Saxo-Tinkoff), Alejandro Valverde (Movistar), Andy Schleck (RadioShack-Trek) and Joaquim Rodríguez (Katusha)—all steered clear of the Giro to target the Tour.

When pre-race favorites Wiggins and defending champion Ryder Hesjedal (Garmin-Sharp) abandoned, all Nibali had to do was stay upright on his bike to win the Giro. His most serious challenges came from Urán, who was seventh last year and started the race as a helper for Wiggins, and Evans, a winner of the 2011 Tour, who only decided five weeks beforehand to race with the idea of using the Giro to prepare for the Tour.

Behind them were Michele Scarponi (Lampre-Merida), a perennial podium man beyond his best, and some young guns, such as Carlos Betancur (Ag2r La Mondiale), who were racing their first grand tour.

In sharp contrast, Nibali started working in November to prepare for the Giro, and came with a loaded, dedicated team fully intent on winning the pink jersey.

Nibali's progression as a grand tour rider has also been consistent, steady, and above all, credible.

Since his grand tour debut in 2007, Nibali's never finished worse than 20th in 10 grand tour starts, and he's finished them all. After nibbling at the top 10 with seventh at 2009 Tour de France, his coming out party was 2010, when he rode

The Athlete Biological Passport

The fight against doping relies on several strategies, including the direct testing of athletes as well as evidence gathered in the context of non-analytical doping violations. By combining these strategies, and seeking new ones to address emerging threats, the global fight against doping is more effective.

The typical doping control approach based on line detection of prohibited substance or their metabolites in an athlete's sample remains an effective approach; however it has limitations when an athlete maybe using substances on an intermittent and/or low-dose basis. Furthermore, new substances or modifications of prohibited substances (e.g. designer drugs) maybe difficult to detect by conventional analytical means. In recent years, doping regimes have become much more scientifically planned and have taken advantage of the weaknesses in traditional protocols: This underscores the need for a more sophisticated and complementary strategy to effectively fight doping, namely the Athlete Biological Passport.

"Questions and Answers on Athlete Biological Passport,"
World Anti-Doping Agency, 2011. www.wada-ama.org.

to third in the Giro, helping then-teammate Ivan Basso take pink, and later winning the Vuelta a España. In fact, since 2010, he has won or been on the podium in five of the six grand tours he's started. His lone hiccup was seventh in the 2011 Vuelta.

Last year, en route to third overall, Nibali was the only rider capable of challenging the Sky gauntlet during the 2012 Tour. So his Giro victory against a relatively thin field should hardly come as a surprise for anyone.

And despite winning by more than four minutes, Nibali didn't do anything that seemed so extraordinary as to provoke guffaws from the peanut gallery.

Nibali's attacks were measured, precise, and relatively short. His stage-winning attack at Tre Cime di Lavaredo on Saturday came less than two kilometers from the tape, and he even later admitted he went too early and was running out of steam.

In today's science-based, number-crunching peloton, perhaps the most telling evidence of Nibali's performance lies in the power meter.

While teams and riders are loath to give away the power numbers of their top riders, La Gazzetta dello Sport published a story revealing some interesting data about Nibali's performance.

La Gazzetta didn't cite the source of the numbers, but even at face value they provided some telling stats. The last time the Giro climbed Tre Cime, Riccardo Riccò and Di Luca were the main protagonists. Riccò, who has since been banned 12 years for illegal blood transfusions, won the stage while Di Luca cemented his grip on the pink jersey. Di Luca, after tackling three other categorized climbs, climbed the final four kilometers of the Tre Cime climb, with an average grade of 12.26 percent, in 15:30. Nibali, while racing in a snowstorm, was 2:30 slower. Using the measure of VAM (vertical meters climbed per hour), Di Luca hit 1,780 VAM in 2007 up Tre Cime, while Nibali posted 1,533 VAM up Tre Cime with 5.29 watts/kg.

Citing Nibali's numbers on the other major climbs, La Gazzetta also estimated that he climbed the last 10km of the Montasio climb in 29:49, with 5.05 watts/kg. Those numbers were challenged by none other than Ferrari, who pegged Nibali's power up the Montasio climb at a whopping 6.4 watts/kg.

Going back to *La Gazzetta's* numbers, up the Jafferau, where he attacked in the final two kilometers in the cold above Bardonecchia, Nibali posted an average of 340 watts during the 7km climb.

The style of racing during this Giro was in marked contrast to 2007 when Riccò and Di Luca were trading punches. Gone are the days when riders would jump clear in the big ring with two climbs to go to a beyond-category summit finish. Nibali's surges at Bardonecchia and Tre Cime both came within 2km of the line.

All of those factors seem to indicate that Nibali won because he was the best prepared, had the best team to support him, didn't suffer any serious health problems or crashes, and arrived at the Giro at the peak of a long and steady trajectory over the past half-decade. There is no proof to indicate anything else, at least not now.

A Nibali positive would be devastating not only for Italian cycling and the Giro, but also for a scandal-ravaged sport desperate to rebuild its credibility. It's hard to imagine that Nibali or Astana would risk everything, knowing the stakes involved, not only for themselves, but also for the larger sport as a whole. However, given the events of the last 24 months on the doping front, a pledge of this nature lacks the weight it held following the Festina Affaire or even Operación Puerto.

Is it a sucker's bet to believe that Nibali might have won the Giro clean? No one wants to be caught with pie on their face again, but until we hear otherwise, Nibali deserves the benefit of the doubt.

Periodical and Internet Sources Bibliography

The following articles have been selected to supplement the diverse views presented in this chapter.

Christie Aschwanden	"The Top Athletes Looking for an Edge and the Scientist Trying to Stop Them," *Smithsonian*, July–August 2012.
Jim Donaldson	"How About One Strike and You're Out for Good?," *Providence Journal*, August 17, 2013.
Stephen Downes	"Drugs and Sport: A Match Made in Heaven," The Age, May 7, 2013.
Malcolm Gladwell	"Man and Superman," *New Yorker*, September 9, 2013.
Aaron Gulley	"Why I Choose to Believe They're Clean," *Outside*, June 7, 2013.
Tommy McCormick	"Steroid Use Is Never Justifiable," *Spartan Daily*, February 12, 2013.
Hector Quesada	"Athletes Should Not Have to Be Role Models," *Collegiate Times*, January 29, 2013.
Jeff Seidel	"Journey to Baseball Hall of Fame Shouldn't Include Steroids," *Detroit Free Press*, July 2, 2013.
Kate Smart	"From a Doping Culture to a Clean Culture," The Roar, October 15, 2012.
Brandon Sneed	"Your Kids Don't Care That Their Favorite Athlete Did Steroids," *Pacific Standard*, August 2, 2013.
Leigh Steinberg	"Why Do We Make Athletes Role Models?," *Forbes*, January 20, 2013.

**OPPOSING
VIEWPOINTS®
SERIES**

CHAPTER 4

How Should Doping Athletes Be Treated?

Chapter Preface

The National Baseball Hall of Fame and Museum was founded in Cooperstown, New York, in 1939 to honor the greatest baseball players, umpires, managers, and executives in the history of the game. In 2013 thirty-seven candidates were considered for induction, and none of them were chosen. It was the first time since 1996 that no candidates were elected. Many observers predicted the outcome, because many of the candidates were suspected of doping. ESPN.com commentator Tim Kurkjian noted at the time that inducting candidates in the future "will become more cumbersome, more awkward and more impossible than ever. And it likely will remain that way for another 25 years, until someone finds a better way to deal with this [steroid] era and the hundreds of players who used performance-enhancing drugs during it."

Many of the candidates nominated for 2013 played baseball during the steroid era, a period from the late 1980s through the late 2000s during which many professional baseball players used steroids. Although Major League Baseball established a ban on performance-enhancing drugs (PEDs) in 1991, the league did not start testing until 2003. For more than a decade, PED use was widespread throughout baseball. Several of the league's leading players during that period have admitted to using them.

During the steroid era, many of baseball's top power hitters racked up unprecedented home run totals, with several of them surpassing the fifty home run mark. In 1998 Mark McGwire and Sammy Sosa became engaged in a home-run race, transfixing the baseball world and shattering the existing home run record. By the end of the season, McGwire had won the competition by hitting seventy home runs; Sosa ended the season with sixty-six. Both players surpassed the 1961 record of sixty-one set by Roger Maris.

Just three years later, Barry Bonds surpassed McGwire's home run record with seventy-three home runs during the 2001 season. However, by this time there was widespread suspicion that several players were doping, including Bonds, McGwire, and Sosa. Sportswriters were quick to question Bonds's achievement, pointing out that he had not surpassed the fifty home run plateau in any previous season. It was clear to many sportswriters and fans that PED use was having a major impact on Major League Baseball.

In the following years, these suspicions were confirmed. Other players from this era would also—fairly or unfairly—be associated with the use of PEDs. This chapter considers how doping athletes should be treated and discusses doping amnesty, the formation of a truth and reconciliation committee, and harsher sanctions versus more prevention and regulation.

| "Clearly current anti-doping control efforts are not producing effective enough controls and disincentives to doping."

There Should Be Much Harsher Sanctions Against Doping in Sports

Neil B.

In the following viewpoint, Neil B. debates whether doping in sports is a moral or legal consideration. He contends that there are some cycling officials who want there to be legal and criminal consequences for doping violations, because the threat of imprisonment and financial ruin may provide an incentive for athletes to remain clean. Neil B. concludes that the governing bodies of sports need to establish harsher antidoping regulations. Neil B. is a contributor to the website Tribesports.

As you read, consider the following questions:

1. According to Neil B., what cycling association was considering putting a legal framework behind the control of doping?

2. What cyclist won gold in the men's cycling road race at the 2012 Olympics, according to Neil B.?

3. What American boxer does Neil B. say supports the idea of legalizing doping in sports?

Recently doping in sport has been thrust into the media and public spotlight more than ever. The Lance Armstrong doping scandal [an investigation proved the American cyclist and others used performance-enhancing drugs; in 2012 Armstrong was stripped of his seven Tour de France titles] has opened the sportsmanship debate up worldwide. While it had long been suspected that doping was rife in sports such as international cycling, the revelations the USADA (United States Anti-Doping Agency) report into Lance Armstrong and cycling brought doping to the forefront of people's thoughts. The shocking truths about the depths of doping and deception Armstrong and many others had gone to, and the years spent vehemently denying these accusations presented an important consideration. Is doping in sports a moral or legal consideration? Is it purely a question of moral sportsmanship or should there be more serious, legal implications to doping? The fact that Armstrong repeatedly sued people who accused him of doping, hitting them both financially and career-wise, is a whole other level of moral debate, that I won't go into in this article. However, the question remains; should doping in sport be a moral or legal issue?

A Legal Framework

The debate as to whether doping should just be a moral question of sportsmanship and fair play, or should be taken into the legal realm was brought to a head in February [2013] when it emerged that Cycling Australia [the national administrative body for cycling in Australia] was considering putting a legal framework behind the control of doping. They propose to have riders sign a statutory declaration about doping, with the potential for criminal prosecution for those who are found to have lied. This legal framework and the possibility to prosecute dopers would completely change the system of doping control. While currently doping is considered a moral consideration, whereby those who dope fall well below standards of sportsmanship and fair play required and expected in sport, and thus can be banned from competing; a change like this would shift the goalposts altogether. The threat of imprisonment and financial ruin that such a legal framework could provide may produce a more effective method of policing doping in sport. Clearly current anti-doping control efforts are not producing effective enough controls and disincentives to doping.

However, there are a number of factors to consider when discussing the issue of doping as either a moral or legal issue. Firstly there is the issue of whether doping in sport should be dealt with from a legal point of view at all. Does a doping offense warrant criminal sanctions? How can you justify it becoming part of the legal sphere? Leading sports law lawyer Gregory Ioannides has argued that there is justification for the application of criminal law for anti-doping violations due to the theory of "public interest", whereby not only can doping be dangerous to the athletes involved, but it is also dangerous and destructive to society. He argues that the application of criminal law on doping in sport has a moral element; but because it is not enforcing the morality of a "political or elitist will", but is enforcing the will of society, it wouldn't be prejudice against any minorities or individuals and so is applicable in law. As such, proceeding with legal action in relation to doping in sport is acting in the public interest, therefore a state, rather than private governing body should be allowed to pass legal judgement.

Rethinking Punishment

Even if doping in sport was to remain purely a moral consideration and continue to be overseen by governing bodies, rather than a legal consideration, there is surely more scope to enforce harsher regulations to make the disincentives to cheat-

Rule Violations by US Athletes, 2012

	1st Quarter	2nd Quarter	3rd Quarter	4th Quarter	Total
Doping Violations	5	7	14	11	37
Whereabouts Failure— Filing Failure	77	86	73	43	279
Whereabouts Failure— Missed Test	1	0	0	2	3

TAKEN FROM: US Anti-Doping Agency, 2013.

ing far stronger. In the recent London 2012 Olympics, we saw an example of someone who had previously been found guilty of doping, competing and winning a gold medal in the Men's Cycling Road Race. Alexander Vinokourov, from Kazakhstan, claimed Gold in the Road Race, despite previously serving a two-year ban for blood-doping in 2007. Similarly, Dwain Chambers was back competing for Great Britain, despite previously having been banned for using the designer steroid THG. Admittedly, the British Olympic Association had tried to enforce a lifetime ban on drug cheats, but this was overturned by the Court of Arbitration for Sport, as it went against World Anti-Doping Agency (WADA) code.

Surely more can be done from a purely moral regulatory standpoint. If every athlete was aware that getting caught using banned substances or techniques would result in a lifetime ban from sport, far more athletes would think twice about doping. Clearly there is more than just the athlete to consider in many doping cases, with pressure coming from outside influences, but fundamentally, if an athlete knows they will be banned for life for doping, then they are less likely to do it.

The Campaign to Legalize Doping

There are also those who argue that the only way doping in sport can be effectively controlled is to legalize it. By legalizing doping in sport, governing bodies would be able to keep track of what doping was happening and would stop the underground production of potentially dangerous drugs. These people argue that if doping was open to everyone, then it creates a fairer playing field than there currently is, as it then becomes available to everyone, so the playing field will be levelled. Indeed American heavyweight boxer Tony Thompson, a man who has fought for world titles on two occasions, recently commented that he thought drugs should be made legal in sport. However, I personally wholeheartedly disagree with this viewpoint. This would actually increase the pressure on athletes to dope, as more people would be doping. This immediately puts those who refuse to dope at a significant disadvantage and could ultimately lead to a two way split in sport, between doping and non-doping athletes. On top of this, it would also completely devalue and destroy the integrity of sport and take away one of the key reasons why people love sport so much.

Sport is about watching athletes at the peak of physical performance; a level that they have achieved through hard work and determination and most of all with integrity and sportsmanship; athletes like [Jamaican sprinter] Usain Bolt. They have reached levels most amateur sportsmen could only dream of reaching, and it is the fact that they have done so in a moral, clean and sportsmanlike way that makes it such an amazing spectacle. Legalizing doping, although it may give some of the control back to the governing bodies, would in my opinion completely devalue the whole concept of "sport" and "competing".

A Hot Debate

Whether or not doping in sport is purely a moral or legal consideration will be a debate that will rage on and on. Furthermore, whether making doping a legal consideration is enforceable or not has still to be fully determined and of course there are lots of areas that need to be considered that this article has not even touched upon. However, it is my opinion that, even if legal sanctions cannot be introduced into antidoping regulations, then far stricter sanctions need to be imposed by governing bodies. An athlete should be under no illusions that committing doping offences will result in the end of their careers as an athlete, as well as all of those involved in facilitating the doping. Sport is sport, because of the sportsmanship, fair play, hard work and determination involved in getting to the top. If doping is not clamped down on or it is legalized, then the fundamental draw of competitive sports is removed. However, while significant efforts have gone into fighting doping in sport, an effective anti-doping regulatory regime has yet to be established as there are still many athletes who are doping going undetected for far too long. Clearly it is an incredibly difficult thing to attempt to police and catching everyone that chooses to dope seems an almost impossible task. However, this should in no way mean that a completely doping free sporting world should not continually be strived for. I for one, believe that imposing far stricter penalties on those who do dope, would represent a significant step forward in the fight against doping in sports.

"Getting behind fairer and safer sport is one thing; openly supporting broader, arguably unfair, punitive trends is another."

Punishing Doping Athletes Isn't a Long-Term Solution

Kate Henne

In the following viewpoint, written in September 2012, Kate Henne posits that there is too much focus on punishment for doping violations and too little focus on prevention. She suggests that antidoping activists should consider the implications of harsh punishments. For some athletes, it means that lifelong dreams and livelihoods are threatened. In extreme cases it can mean a prison sentence. Henne concludes that it would be much more effective to balance the use of punishment with other proactive and responsive measures in order to encourage athletes to reject doping. Kate Henne is a research fellow at the Regulatory Institutions Network at Australian National University in Australia.

As you read, consider the following questions:

1. According to Kate Henne, who was the judge presiding over Lance Armstrong's lawsuit against the United States Anti-Doping Agency?

2. According to Henne, how long of a prison sentence did Marion Jones serve for perjury after admitting to doping?

3. How many antidoping violations does Henne say were caught by the biological passport system just days before the 2012 Olympic Games?

There has been much discussion in recent weeks about Lance Armstrong, his legacy, and charges levelled by the United States Anti-Doping Agency (USADA) that the Texan cyclist spearheaded a systematic doping regime over many years.

By opting out of the USADA arbitration process, Armstrong faces a lifelong suspension from competing, coaching or holding any official position in professional cycling, and has been stripped of his seven Tour de France titles.

But now the dust has settled, what can the Armstrong case tell us about anti-doping regulation in cycling and in sport more generally? Is there too much focus on punishment for "dopers" and too little focus on prevention? And perhaps more importantly, what are the effects of prioritising punishment?

Recent media commentaries have accused USADA of hypocrisy, arguing that the agency charged with protecting "fair play" in sport acted unethically by abusing legal processes and taxpayer dollars to ensure Armstrong's punishment. Others, including James Heathers on The Conversation, have pointed to the mismanagement of drug control.

The judge presiding over Armstrong's lawsuit against USADA, Sam Sparks, has also questioned USADA's motives and ability to work with other governing bodies to regulate and promote cycling.

These criticisms are worth taking seriously.

Having studied the anti-doping regime since 2007, I can attest that nearly every anti-doping official I have met has said that "catching" Armstrong would be the anti-doping movement's crowning achievement. Many of them have stated that changes to the World Anti-Doping Code that took effect in 2009 (such as the requirements for governments detailed in Article 22) would finally make it possible to catch Armstrong.

Citing the growing number of signatories to the UNESCO International Convention Against Doping in Sport, anti-doping officials often contend that increasing government support will ensure more resources for the fight against doping and more punishments.

And they are right. Well, sort of.

Before USADA brought its latest fight to Armstrong, the US Department of Justice had been investigating the Texan. But in February this year, the Department of Justice closed its two-year investigation for reasons that, although still unclear, suggest there was not enough evidence to criminally convict him.

While USADA put together a case against Armstrong, it still couldn't "catch" him in the way that many regulators I have spoken with had hoped.

Anti-doping officials had expressed to me a desire for severe punishments, some going so far as to say Armstrong deserved something akin to what US sprinter Marion Jones endured.

In 2007, Jones lost her Olympic gold medals and lucrative sponsorships, and served a six-month prison sentence for perjury after finally admitting to doping. In contrast, Armstrong is largely unaffected.

With that in mind, it's worth asking if those levels of punishment are really what the anti-doping advocates should want. Jones spent much of her prison sentence in solitary confinement and is a disenfranchised felon for the rest of her life.

A mother of three, she cannot vote, and she cannot be employed in many workplaces—except, luckily, the Women's National Basketball Association. Getting behind fairer and safer sport is one thing; openly supporting broader, arguably unfair, punitive trends is another.

Stepping back to consider these implications is important. While I have yet to meet a professional or aspiring professional cyclist who thinks Armstrong did not dope, there is something more troubling behind his case: a global, anti-doping regime structured to favour punishment, negating opportunities for more responsive regulation.

And by responsive regulation, I mean attempts to balance the use of punishment with meaningful modes of persuasion.

Recently, the Biological Passport system—which monitors athletes' "biological variables" over time—yielded nine anti-doping violations just days before the London Olympic Games.

More generally over the years, the Court of Arbitration in Sport has overwhelmingly ruled against athletes appealing anti-doping violations.

During my own research in Australasia and the United States, I have witnessed many athletes—particularly young men from working-class and ethnic minority backgrounds who perceive sport as a viable career pathway—receive lengthy bans for relatively minor and non-performance-enhancing substance use.

Dreams and livelihoods are jeopardised, because anti-doping regulation takes a punitive stance—sometimes even more so than the national justice system—rather than adopting more proactive or culturally sensitive measures.

Marion Jones

Sprinter and long jumper . . . Marion Jones has gone from enjoying the accolades heaped on the world's fastest female athlete to facing the harsh consequences of using illegal performance-enhancing drugs. By the time she was twenty-two years old, Jones was considered the number-one female athlete in track and field, an achievement made all the more remarkable by the fact it was her first year of competition in the sport. From the basketball court to the track and the long-jump pit, Jones sailed, seemingly effortlessly, to success in all of her athletic endeavors. Speculation regarding her use of performance-enhancing drugs surfaced during her appearance in the 2000 Olympic Games in Sydney, Australia. She vehemently denied using steroids and tested negative for them, but by late 2007 she admitted to using the drugs and has since been stripped of her five Olympic medals. In January of 2008 Jones, with her athletic legacy in ruins, was sentenced to six months in prison on charges of perjury.

"Marion Jones," Biography in Context Online Collection. *Detroit, MI: Gale, 2010.*

While the case against Armstrong points to regulatory shortcomings, it may also be a mistake to suggest his case is indicative of the global regime. I have encountered many zealous anti-doping advocates, but I have met just as many administrators committed to helping athletes navigate the complex web of rules woven by the World Anti-Doping Agency (WADA).

Currently, international rules actually limit local agencies' abilities to deliver specialised programming, in part because responsive authorities commit many resources to help athletes comply with WADA's guidelines.

In the aftermath of Armstrong's case and the actions taken by USADA, it seems timely to ask whether (and how) resources can be more effectively channelled in proactive and responsive ways.

To date, the legacies of anti-doping regulation are not fairer or safer sport, merely an expanding list of athletes punished for violating the rules.

Some athletes have genuinely doped but, at least in my experience, the majority have been duped by a system charged with preventing and deterring doping in sport.

VIEWPOINT 3

> *"If nothing else, getting riders who doped and others who helped them to confess to a truth commission could perhaps be cathartic, both for them and their sport."*

There Should Be a Truth and Reconciliation Committee for Doping Athletes

John Leicester

In the following viewpoint, John Leicester suggests that setting up a truth commission for professional cycling may be necessary for the sport to move past its doping scandals, clear up suspicion, and reestablish itself as a clean sport. He explains that while cycling officials believe such a committee would be difficult to execute, many argue that it is essential if cycling is to move forward and regain the trust of fans all over the world. John Leicester is an international sports columnist for the Associated Press.

As you read, consider the following questions:

1. According to John Leicester, what former pro cyclist is a vocal supporter of a truth and reconciliation committee for doping in cycling?

2. How many former teammates of Lance Armstrong's testified against him to the United States Anti-Doping Agency, according to Leicester?

3. What key cycling figure does Leicester identify as opposing the idea of a truth commission for cycling?

The truth, some say, sets you free. Could it do the same for cycling, help the sport get back in the saddle and move past the damage done by [American cyclist] Lance Armstrong?

It's certainly an interesting idea, perhaps even a good one. Flush out cycling's dirty secrets, rinse them all away. Find out who else doped and how they did it, and then close those loopholes to make it harder for riders, now and in the future, to copy their cheating methods, use their doping doctors and be pressured to dope by old-school team managers.

Addressing a Doping Culture

Something, maybe, not unlike the Truth and Reconciliation Commission that post-apartheid South Africa established to confront and forgive its brutal history. Offer amnesty to those who volunteer information about doping, and tough punishments for continuing to harbor cheats and lies.

Having unmasked Armstrong as a drug cheat, the U.S. Anti-Doping Agency is pushing the sport to take this next step to "fully unshackle itself from the past," uncover doping doctors, corrupt team directors, and riders with doping histories it says remain hidden, undermining any convincing cleanup.

"The past is going to dig itself up, so why not boldly address it?" USADA CEO Travis Tygart said Wednesday [2012] in a phone interview. "You have to give this sport a fresh start."

Among those who support the idea—and, for the moment, it is nothing more than that—is Jonathan Vaughters, who rode with Armstrong as a pro. Vaughters testified to

Apartheid in South Africa

In 1994 the African National Congress (ANC) took over the government of South Africa, officially ending apartheid, the country's policy of racial segregation. The ANC instituted nationwide reforms to promote equality, civil rights, and economic prosperity for all South Africans and in the years that followed many advances were made. The legacy of racism, though, remained firmly entrenched in the nation's economy. In the first decade of the twenty-first century, the majority of black South Africans were as poor, or poorer, than they had been under apartheid policies.

Apartheid was the official government policy in South Africa from 1948 to 1994. During that time, the white South African government passed a number of laws that deprived blacks, coloureds (people of mixed ancestry), and Asians of basic rights—taking away their property and political rights and restricting their movement and activities. Many black South Africans were moved to reserves called homelands, where they were expected to develop their own self-governing societies. But the homelands consisted of poor quality lands with insufficient resources, and residents lived in extreme poverty.

"Apartheid: Lingering Issues,"
Global Issues in Context Online Collection.
Detriot, MI: Gale, 2013.

USADA about doping on their former U.S. Postal Service team, including his own. He is a cycling mover and shaker, running a pro team, Garmin-Sharp-Barracuda, and he was among the thousands who packed a Paris auditorium for Wednesday's unveiling of the Tour route for 2013. Judging from the size and enthusiasm of the crowd, cycling's showcase race still has ample appeal, despite the disgrace of the rider who was its most successful champion.

If nothing else, getting riders who doped and others who helped them to confess to a truth commission could perhaps be cathartic, both for them and their sport. But Vaughters wants it to be more ambitious than that.

"Of course, your objective is absolute truth, but what you are after is trying to figure out where things went wrong and where it can be improved," he said in an interview. "It's not just so that people will be truthful just for the hell of it, to get the monkey off their back. That's a bit useless."

Amnesty

Because people aren't "just going to walk up to you and say 'Hey, by the way, guess what I did,'" the first step would be to declare an amnesty period—a year, month, week, whatever— where past doping is "forgiven totally" to encourage confessions, Vaughters said.

"There has to be an absolute amnesty, otherwise why will people be honest with you?"

Then the commission has to dig and probe, interview people individually, "look for specific rumors or issues or whatever else that seems unaddressed and then try to address them," he said. "You know: 'What happened there? What happened here? We've heard this rumor of X, Y or Z. Is it true? Is it not true?'

"The point of it is that you're trying to figure out what went wrong, how did people avoid testing positive, how did they circumvent anti-doping measures, and so how can that be prevented in the future."

A Cloud of Suspicion

That this idea is being kicked around and will be discussed by the International Cycling Union at a meeting on Friday is, in itself, a measure of how cycling's doping past is hard to shake off. Anti-doping controls are better now than in Armstrong's era and yet suspicion, justified or not, weighs on riders and others who work in the sport today.

The 11 former teammates of Armstrong who testified to USADA identified other people who were involved in doping, but many of those names were blacked out in affidavits the agency published. Do they still work in cycling? If it could answer that, a truth commission would do some good.

Tygart said that during the probe of Armstrong and doping on his teams, USADA uncovered information on "several dozen" other people, some of them still in cycling and so far unidentified. "That's just what we found, there are far more there," he said.

If there's no truth commission, USADA would turn over that information to other anti-doping agencies and the World Anti-Doping Agency.

"It's really important people are revealed," he said. "If you got away with it in the past and think you can get away with it today, what's going to change?"

"There's really no choice."

Obstacles to a Truth Commission

There are hurdles that would need to be overcome for a truth commission to become more than just an idea. Not the least is Pat McQuaid, the cycling federation president who this week rubber-stamped USADA's decision to ban Armstrong for life and erase his seven Tour titles. McQuaid initially appeared interested in an amnesty within cycling but now seems skeptical that South Africa's experience can be translated to cycling.

"Where you've got a white population and a black population who're killing each other over a number of years, that's one thing," the London *Guardian* [newspaper] quoted him as saying this week. "Whether it works in anti-doping or sport is another question. You have to ask yourself, if you can set it up, who's going to give information? Are riders and managers going to come forward? I don't know. Will it stop people wanting to cheat? If they come forward—and that's a big 'if'—will it help much in the future?"

World Anti-Doping Agency rules don't allow for amnesty programs for repenting dopers, although Tygart said that shouldn't be an insurmountable obstacle to establishing a truth commission.

"The need for it is so great, you can work through the details to make it happen," he said.

"It is unchartered territory for the anti-doping community," WADA director general David Howman said by email. But he added that the agency's board "might be interested to hear from any sport" that presents the idea.

"The execution is certainly difficult," Vaughters said.

But so, too, is living with the idea that Armstrong was far from alone in an era ruined by doping, that there are other secrets that need to be uncovered.

The truth could help free cycling from that.

| "*The Tour [de France] has moved from being the greatest test of human endurance to a petty media-fest of allegations, recriminations and scandals, with the world's best athletes being expelled.*"

There Should Be a Doping Amnesty

Julian Savulescu and Bennett Foddy

In the following viewpoint, Julian Savulescu and Bennett Foddy contend that the antidoping mindset in professional cycling is a witch hunt and accuse the United States Anti-Doping Agency of ruining the sport of cycling. They recommend that antidoping laws be relaxed and that an amnesty be put in place for athletes who have violated doping bans in the past. Savulescu and Foddy further recommend that cycling implement a monitoring system that allows athletes to dope safely and with limitations. Julian Savulescu is the director of the Uehiro Centre for Practical Ethics, the Oxford Centre for Neuroethics, and the Institute for Science and Ethics at Oxford University. Bennett Foddy is the deputy director and a senior research fellow at the Institute for Science and Ethics at Oxford University.

As you read, consider the following questions:

1. According to Julian Savulescu and Bennett Foddy, what substance did Alberto Contador test positive for?

2. How much did the average speed of Tour de France racers increase from 1989 to 2005, according to Savulescu and Foddy?

3. What do Savulescu and Foddy recommend for steroid and growth hormone use in athletic competition?

The anti-doping witch hunt being perpetrated by the US Anti-Doping Agency (USADA) is ruining cycling. There is a simple solution: an amnesty for dopers and relax anti-doping laws.

The Story So Far

[American cyclist] Lance Armstrong has accused the USADA of running a vendetta amidst claims from a Dutch newspaper that 4 former team mates are witnesses against him, all of whom are riding in this year's [2012] Tour de France. Speculation on what was offered to these riders in exchange from their testimony has focused on a six month ban, delayed until after the Tour de France, though this has been denied. USADA has refused to name any of the 10 witnesses. Lance Armstrong, in a tweet, has labelled the anonymity and immunity offered in exchange for testimony against him as "selective prosecution" and a "vendetta".

Armstrong stands accused of doping violations between 1998 and 2005, and, if found guilty, will face losing all his seven wins, with accusations including the use of EPO, blood transfusions and steroids, following his treatment for cancer [Armstrong was diagnosed with testicular cancer in 1996] and throughout his Tour de France wins. His former team mates [George] Hincapie, [Levi] Leipheimer, [Christian] Vande Velde and [David] Zabriskie did not stand for consideration for the

United States Olympic team. A two year federal investigation resulted in no charges filed and Armstrong has not failed any drug tests but has been dogged by rumours and accusations for many years.

The fact is though that every winner of the Tour de France has been implicated in doping since [Spaniard] Miguel Indurain, except [Australian] Cadel Evans and [Luxembourger] Andy Schleck.

Alberto Contador

Over 18 months after the race, [Spaniard] Alberto Contador was recently stripped of his 2010 Tour de France title, and banned for 2 years by the Court of Arbitration for Sport, making Andy Schleck the winner of the 2010 race.

Contador's ban is punishment for the traces of clenbuterol, an anabolic steroid, found in his blood. Initially cleared by the Royal Spanish Cycling Federation back in February 2011, Contador blamed the traces on contaminated meat brought in by a friend—indeed the traces were small—40 times lower than the minimum rate WADA [World Anti-Doping Agency] insists labs must be able to register to gain accredited status. However, it is possible that Contador was blood doping using blood taken during a training phase that had been insufficiently washed, leaving traces of steroids behind. Plasticizers were also found in his blood and can be a sign of IV usage, though the doctor who invented the test believes these tests may not yet be legally binding. [American cyclist] Floyd Landis was also excluded with a similar pattern of steroid detected during the final stages of the race, probably as a result of contaminated blood doping.

[Belgian cyclist] Eddy Merckx said at the time of Contador's ban to Eurosport [a European television network]: "Sad for him and cycling. I think someone wants the death of cycling. We're going too far."

A Disturbing Trend

In the 2007 Tour de France race leader and likely eventual winner, [Dane] Michael Rasmussen, was sacked a few stages from the end on an allegation of doping (without evidence). Pre-race favourite [Russian Alexander] Vinokourov was expelled after blood doping and his team Astana withdrew. The Cofidis team withdrew from the Tour de France following the news that their Italian rider Cristian Moreni tested positive for testosterone. The eventual winner was in fact the now-convicted drug doper, Contador, and this victory has not been affected by his recent ban.

The Tour has moved from being the greatest test of human endurance to a petty media-fest of allegations, recriminations and scandals, with the world's best athletes being expelled like shabby contestants in [the television show] *Big Brother*.

For the competitors, doping is a part of the spirit of Le Tour. Since it began in 1903, riders have invariably used performance-enhancing substances in an attempt get through the gruelling 21 day test of human endurance. They have taken alcohol, caffeine, cocaine, amphetamines, steroids, growth hormone, EPO [erythropoietin] and blood doping. [Italian] Fausto Coppi, who won the golden jersey in 1949 and 1952, summed it up when he was asked whether he ever used amphetamines, or "La Bomba", and replied, "Only when absolutely necessary." When asked how often that was, he said, "Most of the time."

The 1967 Tour saw English rider [Tom] Simpson collapse and die during the competition with amphetamines in his pocket.

The Tour requires a superhuman effort. [Dane] Bjarne Riis, 1996 Tour winner, admitted taking EPO. The 1997 winner, [German] Jan Ullrich, was later alleged to be taking drugs. Floyd Landis, 2006 winner, was disqualified testing positive for testosterone.

A Doping Culture

Looking at the ranking of the 10th Stage of Tour de France 2005 (Grenoble-Courchevel), Verner Moller in his excellent book, *The Scapegoat* notes that of the first 25 riders placed on that stage, only seven are still uncompromised by doping allegations or convictions. And only one in the top 17 (Cadel Evans) is untainted.

Indeed with the ever increasing speed of the Tour de France, some riders have claimed it is now impossible without doping. In 1989, when advances were made in bike technology, average speed was 37.5kph. In 2005, it was 40.9kph, an increase of over 8%. Moller explains these apparently small increases in speed mask a large increase in effort—8% increase in speed means 16% more air must be moved, means 16% more energy is required to go 8% faster. In the context of a race won by seconds, by athletes at the top of their abilities, this is a huge increase.

[German Jörg] Jaksche, an ex-cyclist who has confessed doping, but after 1998 scandals rode 1999 clean, described his experience riding without enhancement:

> "You hope from day-to-day that the speed goes down. You have to push yourself harder and your recuperation is slower, there was no way I could hang on, and I felt completely superfluous. In the end I was afraid of being left behind on a railway bridge." He explains the catch-22: "Only the one who dopes wins. Only the one who wins appears in the media. Only the one in the media makes the sponsor happy. Only happy sponsors invest new money in the team the following year."

The Solution

Based on the obvious and abundant evidence, it would be unusual if a winner of the Tour today could recurrently win the Tour without doping. Of course it is possible but it is highly

Anabolic Steroids

Anabolic steroids, which increase strength by building muscle mass, can be naturally occurring or synthetically produced. Anabolic steroids also help athletes recover from injury more quickly. Performance-enhancing anabolic steroids include testosterone, the male sexual hormone, and other similarly structured steroids, including stanozolol, dihydrotestosterone, androstenedione (commonly known as Andro), dehydroepiandrosterone, clostebol, and nandrolone. At the 1988 Olympics, Canadian sprinter Ben Johnson was stripped of his gold medal and world record in the 100m (one hundred-meter sprint race) after he tested positive for the steroid stanozolol.

Steroids have several legitimate medical applications, including hormone replacement therapy, bone marrow stimulation, growth stimulation, and muscle preservation for patients with chronic wasting diseases. Athletes who use steroids to enhance athletic performance may experience numerous undesirable and dangerous side effects, including mood swings and aggression (commonly referred to as roid rage), depression, liver damage, and infertility or other sexual side effects. Female steroid users may also experience facial and body hair, a deepening of the voice, and altered menstrual cycles.

"Sports and Drug Use,"
Global Issues in Context Online Collection.
Detroit, MI: Gale, 2013.

likely that most, or at least a very substantial proportion, of top level riders and nearly all recent winners of the Tour have been doping.

In such an environment, it achieves nothing worthwhile to attack the legends of the sport. It is arbitrary and unfair to single out high profile dopers from the past when we can't be sure in any reliable way who was and was not doping, especially when all evidence indicates it has been, and probably still is, rife.

It is especially wrong to persecute past dopers when there is a better and obvious solution.

First, we need to stop all investigations into past doping. It is past. We can never fully and fairly investigate who was and was not doping in the past. We should create an amnesty for past dopers.

Relax the Ban

Second, we should relax the ban on doping. Much of the fuss in the Tour that is destroying its spectacle and credibility is related to the use of EPO to raise red blood cell levels and increase oxygen carrying capacity. Recently, riders seemed to have turned away from using EPO to using blood doping, transfusing back previously donated blood at that time of a race. Last year, one rider got renal failure from using blood that was too old. Blood doping is virtually impossible to detect.

But we could eliminate this whole problem with the stroke of a pen. If we allowed riders to blood dope up to a haematocrit level of 50% where half their blood would be red blood cells, we could administer a safe, cheap, simple reliable test on all riders. Those over 50% would be out, those under in. There would be no more blood doping scandals. And such a level is already accepted by the international cycling union as safe.

What about other drugs, like steroids, growth hormone etc? Is there also a solution for them?

Addressing the Prohibition Crowd

Three arguments are commonly given in favour of prohibiting the use of any performance-enhancing drug in sporting competition. That the drug is too unsafe. That it perverts the nature and spirit of the sporting competition. And that we should ban the drug simply because it enhances performance.

The last of the three ought to be dismissed out of hand every time it appears. Modern athletic sport is entirely focused on finding new ways to break the old records, and most of the effective methods are legal. Hypoxic training tents, which simulate the effect of training at high altitude by allowing the blood to carry more oxygen, are legal. Caffeine, which improves reaction time and fights fatigue, is legal. So are advanced dietary regimes, which maximize the amount of energy available to the athlete's muscles on the day of competition.

The other two arguments, by contrast, provide us with good reason for banning certain drugs in certain situations. Some drugs do change the nature of a given sport, so that it changes into a less interesting or less valuable pursuit. For example, we tend to think that one of the most interesting things about boxing is that boxers need to overcome their fear of being hit to perform well. If they took a drug that entirely eliminated their ability to feel fear, or pain, this valuable aspect of the performance would be eliminated from the sport. Similarly, when archers or professional pistol shooters use beta-blocker drugs to steady their hands, that removes one of the most interesting aspects of those sports: the challenge of controlling one's nerves.

Do anabolic steroids and growth hormone make cycling and athletic sports like running less interesting? It is hard to see why this would be the case. Steroids enhance performance by allowing athletes to train longer and recover more quickly. They enhance the effect of training. Athletes on steroids still have to train hard, in fact they still have to overcome every challenge faced by their non-doping peers. If every Olympic sprinter or cyclist were using steroids, it would still be the same sport, just slightly faster.

The Danger of PEDs

Finally, there is the argument that drugs need to be banned because they are too dangerous. In the history of competitive sport several exceedingly dangerous drugs have been used to enhance performance. In the third modern Olympic games, the winner of the men's marathon was given strychnine (a lethal poison) during the race as a stimulant. More recently, drugs have appeared that allows athletes to modify their genes to increase the performance of their muscles—but these drugs are nowhere near safe enough for humans, and their side effects are not well understood. It makes sense to ban drugs like these.

However, the dangers of any performance-enhancer need to be put in context. Nothing in life is completely safe, not even drinking water or going for a morning stroll. Athletic sport is especially dangerous—it causes more deaths, both in training and competition, than steroids do, and it produces millions of crippling injuries every year. If a performance-enhancing drug is significantly less dangerous than the training for that sport, or than competing in it, then the dangers of the drug may be so low as to make them insignificant.

In the case of cycling, the dangers of cycling at speeds in excess of 60km/hr vastly outweigh the risks of the use of steroids or growth hormone, when administered by a medical professional.

Anabolic Steroids

Anabolic steroids are nothing more than the synthetic form of the natural hormone, testosterone. To receive a benefit in sporting performance, ordinary athletes need to take a dose of the hormone that would be very unusual in an unenhanced body. But testosterone is not a poisonous substance like strychnine. In its naturally-occurring form it is a natural byproduct of heavy training, and many of its worst side-effects—immune deficiency, enlarged ventricles in the heart, and depression—are also common symptoms of overtraining. In this context, steroids are still dangerous, but perhaps not much more dangerous than hard training and professional full-contact sport.

We have good reason to ban certain kinds of performance enhancing drugs. Boxers should not be able to take strong painkillers during competition, and no athlete should be able to take truly dangerous or untested drugs like the new genetic medicines. But the case against steroids is much weaker.

The biggest problem with anabolic steroids is that they are obtained illegally, and then self-administered in secret by athletes who are not trained to identify overuse or to scale their dose appropriately. Like many behind-the-counter drugs, steroids can be taken safely but it is not safe enough to take them on your own. It would be much safer to take steroids for performance enhancement if they could be administered and monitored by a doctor.

For these reasons, we suggest that the legal shackles are removed from steroid and growth hormone use, and put in the hands of the prescription system. Athletes would be able to obtain steroids from their doctor on request. However, the moral and legal responsibility for the athlete's health would be passed from the athlete, who after all is no expert on modern medicine, to the doctor. Any doctor who overprescribed steroids, or who prescribed any unreasonably dangerous drug, would be struck off the medical register.

We can preserve the nature and spirit of competitive sport as well as the health of athletes, and we can do it within the existing structures of the medical drug schedule and prescription system. Perhaps there is no need for an anti-doping programme at all, in cycling, or indeed in any sport.

> *"When I vote for a player I am upholding him for the highest individual honor possible. My vote is an endorsement of a career."*

Why I'll Never Vote for a Known Steroids User for the Hall of Fame

Tom Verducci

In the following viewpoint, written in January 2013, Tom Verducci explains why he will not vote for any known steroid user for the National Baseball Hall of Fame and Museum in Cooperstown, New York. Verducci argues that voting for a known steroid user is the same as endorsing steroid use, which he will not do because steroids so drastically effect an athlete's performance and produce an uneven playing field. Verducci concludes that the issue is a complicated and difficult one, especially now that players from the steroid era, the period from the late 1980s through the late 2000s during which many professional baseball players used steroids, are beginning to appear on the ballot for consideration. Tom Verducci is an author, journalist, television sports commentator, and writer for Sports Illustrated *magazine.*

As you read, consider the following questions:

1. According to Tom Verducci, approximately how many baseball writers are eligible to vote to induct baseball players into the National Baseball Hall of Fame and Museum?

2. What professional baseball player does Verducci use as an example of a hall of fame candidate with suspicious connections to and attitudes toward steroid use in baseball?

3. Who came up with the idea for the National Baseball Hall of Fame and Museum?

A quarter of a century after the disgrace of Ben Johnson at the Seoul Olympics, more than a decade after the single season home run record was corrupted six times in four years (and not at all in 48 seasons before and since) and in the immediate wake of confirmation that Lance "Never Failed a Test" Armstrong—surprise!—masterminded a massive fraud, I still have to explain why I will not endorse any known steroid user for the Hall of Fame.

First, you must understand the voting process. A ballot is sent to me in the mail—a personal ballot, just as it is sent to about 570 baseball writers eligible to vote. This is not an SAT test or a trivia contest. There are no "right" and "wrong" answers. This one ballot is my judgment. Yes, I am being asked to be "judge" or juror, in the parlance of some writers uncomfortable with responsibility, but I am only one of many hundreds.

When I vote for a player I am upholding him for the highest individual honor possible. My vote is an endorsement of a career, not part of it, and how it was achieved. Voting for a known steroid user is endorsing steroid use. Having spent too much of the past two decades or so covering baseball on the subject of steroids—what they do, how the game was subverted by them, and how those who stayed away from them were disadvantaged—I cannot endorse it.

Based on past statements, such a dismissal is also obvious to many former players, including Hank Aaron, who has said no steroid users should go into the Hall ("The game has no place for cheaters"), Andre Dawson ("Individuals have chosen the wrong road, and they're choosing that as their legacy"), Goose Gossage ("Cheaters should absolutely not be in the Hall of Fame"), Todd Zeile ("Why doesn't anybody see that it's cheating and it's wrong?"), David Wells ("To me, if you've cheated as a player, that's as bad as being a scab") and Dale Murphy ("Everyone understood that it was against the law . . . It was also against the spirit of the game. That's why everybody did it in secret. I have a hard time endorsing that, because there were a lot of guys who decided, 'I'm not going to do that.'")

Where are all the former players arguing for known steroid users to be in the Hall? Anybody?

Listen to what Mark McGwire said in an interview after being hired as the Dodgers hitting coach after last season. McGwire is an admitted steroid user who retired *before any testing took place.*

"It's a mistake that I have to live with for the rest of my life," he said. "I have to deal with never, ever getting into the Hall of Fame. I totally understand and totally respect their opinion and I will never, ever push it. That is the way it's going to be and I can live with that.

"One of the hardest things I had to do this year was sit down with my 9- and 10-year-old boys and tell them what dad did. That was a really hard thing to do but I did it. They understood as much as a 9- or 10-year old could. It's just something, if any ball player ever came up to me, run away from it. It's not good. Run away from it."

McGwire—before or after admission—never has received 25 percent of the BBWAA vote. The threshold for election is

75 percent. I respect the process. If Barry Bonds or Roger Clemens can clear the same bar 112 other electees have cleared since voting began in 1936, I respect that—just as I would even if the consensus leaves nobody enshrined in results announced Wednesday.

Consider this: this ballot is packed with eventual Hall of Famers no matter the Wednesday outcome. How do we know? In the 35 ballots from 1968, when current voting rules were put in place, through 2002, the average ballot included 10.2 eventual Hall of Famers—though only an average of 1.6 per year reached the 75 percent threshold. Those 35 elections never had fewer than five Hall of Famers on the ballot (1995) and had as many as 16 (1969).

(The writers have been fairly consistent in the flow of voting players in. Hall of Famers elected per year by decade since the '70s: 1.3, 1.9, 1.5, 1.7, 1.7).

McGwire's rare words about understanding the impact of steroids on the voting process are admirable. Still, others outside the game offer excuses that McGwire himself doesn't touch. Here are the most popular rationalizations:

1. "It wasn't against the rules."

The conspiracy of silence to this day tells you all you need to know about the hollowness of such a claim. Again, we were a decade outside of the steroid bust of Ben Johnson. Steroids were a well-known taboo. Everyone knew, including those who took them, steroids were a conscious, elaborate, covert decision to go outside the boundaries of fair competition, not to enable performance but to enhance it beyond what was naturally possible.

Pitcher Matt Herges, who said steroids made him "superhuman . . . an android, basically," once said, "We didn't have drug testing anyways. But it was still wrong."

When George Mitchell conducted his white paper investigation into steroids in baseball, his investigators contacted 68 players. Only one of them was willing to talk about steroids:

Dan Naulty, the former Twins and Yankees pitcher whose chilling story I profiled last year. Naulty lived the lie. His debunking of the "it wasn't against the rules" nonsense is as thorough as anything I've ever heard:

"I was a full blown cheater and I knew it," Naulty said. "You didn't need a written rule. I was violating clear principals that were laid down within the rules. Whether they were explicitly stated that I shouldn't use speed or testosterone didn't need to be stated. I understood I was violating mainly implicit principals.

"I have no idea how many guys were using testosterone. But I would assume anybody that was had some sort of conviction that this was against the rules. Look, my fastball went from 87 to 96! There's got to be some sort of violation in that. It was not by natural cause. To say it wasn't cheating to me was . . . it's just a fallacy. There's just no way you could say that's not cheating. It was a total disadvantage to play clean."

2. "Everybody was doing it."

This canard infuriates me the most. When I wrote the 2002 SI investigation on steroids in baseball in which Ken Caminiti said about half the players in the game were juicing, people criticized him for exaggerating the problem. Many of those same people now are using the "everybody was doing it" excuse. It's a lazy, terrible insult to everybody who played the game clean.

The genesis of that article was that during the 2001 season many clean players were complaining to me that steroids had become so prevalent in the game that they felt clearly disadvantaged. That's when I knew the game reached a tipping point: when a few rogue early adopters had grown into hundreds of cheaters. The hundreds who played the game clean were harmed. Many lost jobs, money and opportunity by choosing to play the game clean. I think of them every time I get a Hall of Fame ballot.

As so many writers go to bat for steroid users, the clean players are dismissed as "everybody was doing it" or, "pitchers were doing it, too, so it was an even playing field." Go back and read the story of Naulty and the four Miracles of Fort Myers—three pitchers who played clean were left behind in the minors as Naulty juiced his way to the majors—and tell me about even playing fields.

Never has there been a more uneven playing field since the game was integrated than the one during the Steroid Era.

You have to understand how much steroids changed the game. In the rush to dismiss them, people have thrown out awkward analogies about petroleum jelly, sandpaper, cork, tacks, diet pills from the '70s, etc. under the catchall category of "cheating." Stop it. You know what steroids are like? Steroids. Nothing else rises to the level of steroids when it comes to anabolically changing the body so that it can do far more than it ever could do without them. Steroids took hold because they take a player well beyond his natural ability. Caminiti said he felt like "Superman" with steroids; they even improved his speed.

Beware the player who uses the Mr. Olympia analogy: you know, "if steroids helped baseball players the game would be populated with bodybuilders." It's an awkward cover. The edge players gained was enormous, such as Naulty gaining 68 pounds and 10 miles an hour on his fastball—using steroids only in the offseason, by the way!—or a minor league teammate, Jeff Horn, who said, "A good fastball could get in on me and tie me up. When I had the stuff in me I could get to those pitches easier. With steroids you could do those things you otherwise couldn't do. The things that kept you in the minor leagues all of a sudden didn't hold you back anymore."

Horn bought his steroids off the internet. There are all kinds of steroids with all kinds of purposes that can be combined with all kinds of other drugs. People talk about steroids as if it's one magic pill with the same effect for everyone. The truth is even within the world of steroid cheats there are many levels of unfairness. Take Bonds, for instance, a major league player with world class ability already who, thanks to Game of Shadows, we know engaged in the most sophisticated, state-of-the-art doping regimen ever documented in baseball. Caminiti, on the other hand, bought testosterone in Mexico and, with disastrous effects to his body, self-medicated.

The extrapolation of baseball before Caminiti spoke up was this: the trust in a fair game was being depleted as jobs and games were being decided by who had the best chemist. A parade of players pushed baseball in that direction, and many of the names on this Hall of Fame ballot were not just in the parade but, because of their success, the drum majors leading it.

I do believe players from this era begin with an assumption of innocence. I believe Fred McGriff, for instance, is vastly undersupported in Hall of Fame voting. He retired as only the 10th player with an OPS of .886 or better with more than 10,000 plate appearances. The other nine are a who's who of inner-circle Hall of Famers: Mike Schmidt, Hank Aaron, Frank Robinson, Willie Mays, Stan Musial, Mel Ott, Babe Ruth, Ty Cobb and Tris Speaker. You may ask, "But how do you know he's clean?" I start with a presumption of innocence and then consider any information about connections to steroids. With McGriff, I have come into no such information to move off the presumption.

I try to be fair. Speculation alone is dangerous. I'll use Jeff Bagwell as an example. He's a guy I voted for again. But here are some facts about Bagwell: he hired a bodybuilder (later hired by Luis Gonzalez) in 1995 to make him "as big as I can," flexibility be damned; took the steroid precursor andro (as well as supplements such as creatine, HMB, zinc, etc.), underwent a massive body change; maintained a bodybuilder weightlifting regimen; called the whistle-blowing in 2002 by Caminiti "a shame" and the one in 2005 by Jose Canseco "very disappointing . . . whether it's true or not;" promulgated the red herring that drugs don't help baseball players ("Hand-eye coordination is something you can't get from a bottle," he said of his andro use); and as recently as 2010 in an ESPN interview openly endorsed steroid use by anyone from a fringe player ("I have no problem with that") to superstars such as Bonds and McGwire ("I know you took it but it doesn't matter") as well as the HGH use by an injured Andy Pettitte ("That's not a performance enhancer").

I disrespect his position on steroids and wonder why someone of a bodybuilder mindset who endorses steroid use would walk right up to the steroid line himself without crossing it. His comments, right before his first year on the ballot, bothered me so much that I didn't vote for him that year—I needed more time to process his candidacy, a kind of deferral that is not uncommon. Without subsequent information, I have voted for him since. No, voting isn't easy. This is the kind of toxicity the players left behind from The Steroid Era.

Now use Armstrong as an example when it comes to PED evidence. His defense, even when blasted with 1,000 pages of evidence of PED use by USADA, has remained the same for years and sounds familiar to anybody who has followed the lying steroid users in baseball. His lawyer responded by noting that Armstrong has passed "500–600 tests" and that USADA was on a (here it comes, everybody) "witch hunt" to go after a "retired cyclist." Cue the violins.

Now think about how Armstrong was busted: with no admission, no positive test, no court ruling. (In fact, the US Attorney in Los Angeles only months earlier dropped an investigation into Armstrong's drug use.) Put him on a Hall of Fame ballot and half the writers would vote for him under the "there's no evidence" umbrella.

How was Armstrong, long associated with PED rumors, finally exposed? Teammates. Eleven former teammates finally said the emperor had no clothes. They, too, were dirty. Armstrong didn't just use PEDs, he also instilled and maintained an entire system of corrupt competition, all of it based on a culture of silence and deceit. Sound familiar?

The same lesson applies to baseball. The Steroid Era, too, is an ongoing archeology: buried secrets known to many—teammates, trainers, suppliers, coaches, etc.—that sometimes get revealed with a little brushing away of the topsoil, not always as public as the work of Canseco or Mitchell.

Finally, why should we care at all? Good question. You, in fact, may not care. But this one of 570 or so is my ballot. I do care. One reason is the "character clause" in the voting instructions, something that many writers and observers have mangled out of shape in Cirque du Soleil acrobatics to excuse steroid users. The label "character clause" has become a pejorative. No such title exists. The instructions say only, "Voting shall be based upon the player's record, playing ability, integrity, sportsmanship, character, and contributions to the team(s) on which the player played."

People have twisted this to mean "morals," or, that since "racists" are in the Hall, you must allow steroid users. Such assumptions have led people to promote the idea of removing the "character clause." Do these people know the origin of the clause?

The clause comes from the man who came up with the very idea of the Hall of Fame itself: Alexander Cleland, an immigrant from Scotland who worked for Stephen Clark, a wealthy lawyer who grew up in Cooperstown. After a meeting with Clark in Cooperstown in 1934, Cleland saw laborers working on Doubleday Field and learned from them about plans there five years hence to celebrate the 100th anniversary of the game's mythical beginning. On the train to New York, an inspired Cleland composed a memo to Clark about the idea of a baseball museum in Cooperstown. Later, with the backing of NL president Ford Frick, Cleland and Clark included the idea of enshrining the best players as part of the

America's Game

The appeal of the game [of baseball] had much to do with what many considered its uniquely American origins. "It's our game—that's the chief fact in connection with it: America's game," exclaimed poet Walt Whitman. Baseball, he wrote, "has the snap, go, fling of the American atmosphere—belongs as much to our institutions, fits into them as significantly, as our constitutions, laws: is just as important in the sum total of our historic life." To preserve this patriotic image, baseball administrators such as Albert Spalding and A.G. Mills vehemently dismissed any claims that baseball had evolved from rounders [an English sport]. In 1905, Mills headed a commission to investigate the origins of baseball. The group found that baseball was uniquely American and bore no traceable connection with rounders, "or any other foreign sport." Mills traced the game's genesis to Abner Doubleday in Cooperstown—a sketchy claim, to be sure, as Mills' only evidence rested on the recollections of a boyhood friend of Doubleday who ended his days in an institution for the criminally insane. Still, Doubleday was a war hero and a man of impeccable character, and so the commission canonized the late New Yorker as the founder of baseball, later consecrating ground in his native Cooperstown [New York] for the purpose of establishing the sport's Hall of Fame.

"Baseball,"
St. James Encyclopedia of Popular Culture.
Detroit, MI: Gale, 2000.

museum. They decided to enlist the Baseball Writers Association of America to hold an election in 1936 to decide which players would be so honored.

According to an August 1944 memo by Hall of Fame treasurer Paul Kerr, it was Cleland who listed general rules for voters, including the 75 percent threshold and also deciding that "those worthy of Hall of Fame election should be selected from the ranks for ability, character, and their general contribution to base ball in all respects."

Now you know that one of the founding fathers instructed "character" to be considered from the birth of the Hall itself. It's a central, original principle of the voting process. You don't just dismiss the Thomas Jefferson of the Hall of Fame and 77 years of history to accommodate steroid users.

(Here's an example of why "character" has mattered from the very beginning of Hall elections. In that inaugural 1936 election, 226 baseball writers cast ballots. They could vote for up to 10 candidates, and mostly all did. A total of 2,231 votes were cast, or an average of 9.87 names per ballot. Joe Jackson, a career .356 hitter, received only two of the 2,231 votes. Jackson was fully eligible for Hall of Fame election, though commissioner Kenesaw Mountain Landis had banned him from baseball because of his involvement in the 1919 Black Sox scandal. The writers overwhelmingly decided he was not a Hall of Famer.

Bill Slocum, writing in the *New York American*, immediately took notice of the lack of support for Jackson, who otherwise had the eligibility and the numbers to gain far more support, if not election. Rule 21d, the Major League Baseball rule prohibiting betting on games, wasn't even in place when Jackson was implicated in the Black Sox scandal. Landis crafted it in the early 1920s. The rule prohibiting players on the ineligible list from appearing on a Hall of Fame ballot was not adopted until 1991, as a pre-emptive measure to keep Pete Rose from being considered by the writers.)

Forget the racists and scoundrels comparison. Here's my issue with steroid users as it relates to the "character clause:" it's about how they played the game between the lines, not how they conducted themselves outside of it. It's an issue of competitive integrity, not personal integrity. They bastardized baseball, eroded the implicit fairness of it and disadvantaged those who chose to play fairly to extents never seen before.

McGwire understands he is not getting into the Hall of Fame. Neither are Rafael Palmeiro or Sammy Sosa. Clemens and Bonds are not getting in this year or probably the next few years, though they may gain support as some writers drop their "first ballot" protest non-votes or more come around to think that "they were Hall of Famers before they started juicing," a rationalization I reject. The notion that steroid use is acceptable based on some sliding scale of accomplishment or talent is strange but entirely 21st century American.

Three months before my Hall of Fame ballot arrived, I read a story in the *New York Times* titled "Studies Find More Students Cheating, With High Achievers No Exception." It was about academic fraud. It said nothing about steroids. But I saw steroids in baseball written between the lines, particularly these paragraphs:

> Howard Gardner, a professor at the Harvard Graduate School of Education, said that over the 20 years he has studied professional and academic integrity, "the ethical muscles have atrophied," in part because of a culture that exalts success, however it is attained.

> He said the attitude he has found among students at elite colleges is: "We want to be famous and successful, we think our colleagues are cutting corners, we'll be damned if we'll lose out to them, and some day, when we've made it, we'll be role models. But until then, give us a pass."

Steroid users want the pass, though they remain too shamefully silent to ask for it. I tend to be slightly tougher than average on the Hall of Fame voting scale, but this year voted for six (right around the recent average of the electorate) of the 36 names on the ballot: Bagwell, Craig Biggio, McGriff,

Jack Morris, Tim Raines and Curt Schilling. Next year could present an even harder challenge. With six on my ballot this year, and the possibility of a shutout looming, and Greg Maddux, Tom Glavine, Frank Thomas, Mike Mussina and Jeff Kent all viable first-time 2014 choices, I could have more good choices than available spots. Should the Hall change the rules to allow for more than 10 votes per ballot? It's a legitimate question as the voting has begun to reflect the messiness and complications of the Steroid Era.

| "Baseball is constantly evolving, and the Hall of Fame should honour the players who were most valuable in each era under the rules of the time."

Steroids in Baseball: If You Ain't Cheatin', You Ain't Tryin'

D.R.

In the following viewpoint, written in January 2013, D.R. explains that none of the baseball player candidates on the 2013 ballot for induction into the National Baseball Hall of Fame and Museum in Cooperstown, New York, received enough votes for induction. According to D.R., the candidates did not receive enough votes because they had used, or were suspected of using, steroids during their careers. D.R. concludes that baseball and its rules are constantly changing, so voters should vote for the players who were most valuable under the rules in place during each player's career. D.R. also contends that leaving steroid-using players out of the hall of fame completely is whitewashing history. D.R. is a blogger for Economist *magazine.*

As you read, consider the following questions:

1. When does D.R. say was the last time that no candidates were voted into the National Baseball Hall of Fame and Museum?

2. According to D.R., when did Fay Vincent send out a memorandum to teams announcing that players would be prohibited from using any illegal drugs?

3. On what date did the owners and players agree to institute a new random testing program for HGH, according to D.R?

There will be no joy in Cooperstown, New York, this summer, now that America's mighty priesthood of sportswriters has struck out in its effort to find candidates worthy of induction to the National Baseball Hall of Fame and Museum. Unlike in basketball or American football, sports in which admission to the Hall of Fame is seen merely as a fitting coda to an accomplished career, membership in baseball's shrine, founded in 1936, is universally seen as the game's highest honour. Whether it is because baseball is the oldest of the main North American sports, because the game is so easily measured by statistics, or because it has been touted for so long as the embodiment of American society, its Hall of Fame arouses passions like little else, and the cases of borderline candidates provide an inexhaustible source of spirited debate for fans and pundits. Moreover, the legions of aficionados and dignitaries that descend on the institution's home of Cooperstown— where, according to an entirely apocryphal tale, baseball was invented in 1839—provide an annual economic jolt to the town's myriad memorabilia dealers and hotels. On January 9th the Baseball Writers' Association of America (BBWAA), the group of journalists that the Hall has entrusted to choose its members, announced that for the first time since 1996 and only the eighth time in its history, not a single player was named on at least three-quarters of the 569 ballots, the requirement for election.

The vote was widely seen as a repudiation of the game as it was played during the 1990s and early 2000s, when the use of performance-enhancing drugs (PEDs) such as steroids and human growth hormone (HGH) is now believed to have been rampant. The two greatest players of that era, Barry Bonds and Roger Clemens, both ended their careers in 2007, which meant that following the prescribed five-year waiting period, they made their debuts on the Hall of Fame ballot in this election. There is strong evidence that they used PEDs in their late 30s: government agents investigating illegal steroid dealers found detailed records of Mr Bonds' alleged consumption, and Mr Clemens's former trainer says he personally injected the star pitcher with PEDs. Both players were also tried for perjury for denying they knowingly used PEDs, though neither was convicted. Although their statistical records easily exceed the Hall's established standards, the writers showed them no mercy. Taking advantage of the BBWAA's nebulous guidelines, which stipulate that "voting shall be based upon the player's record, playing ability, integrity, sportsmanship, character, and contributions to the team(s) on which the player played," the electorate gave them just 36% and 37% of the vote.

Suspicions of PED use also dragged down exceptionally strong candidates who have never been tied to steroids. Among the other options on the 2013 ballot were Mike Piazza, the best-hitting catcher in baseball history; Curt Schilling, an elite pitcher who was especially effective in the playoffs that determine the league champion; Craig Biggio, a speedy, consistent second baseman; and Jeff Bagwell, Mr Biggio's powerful teammate. Although none of them were quite as valuable as Mr Bonds or Mr Clemens, they are all historic greats at their positions, and should have coasted to induction. But it seems that the mere chance that one of them might subsequently be revealed to have used PEDs was enough to keep them out.

Needless to say, the voters have shown no consistency over the years regarding which sins disqualify a player from consideration for the Hall. One argument against steroid users is that they behaved immorally, contrary to the Hall's guidelines that members show good character. But such concerns did not lead to the exclusion of players like Cap Anson, who spearheaded the movement to institute racial segregation in baseball, or Ty Cobb, who sharpened the spikes on his cleats in the hopes of injuring opposing players and was known to lunge into the stands to physically attack fans.

Another critique is that PED users only produced Hall of Fame–caliber statistics because they cheated, and that they were thus not truly Hall-worthy talents. However, the same could be said of Gaylord Perry, who not only spent decades throwing a spitball, a pitch which had been banned since 1920, but even wrote a book about it midway through his career. The writers duly elected him to the Hall in 1991. It's hard to imagine that even the best steroids could help as much as illegally doctoring a baseball does for pitchers. Moreover, by the time Mr Bonds and Mr Clemens allegedly began taking steroids, they were already recognised as among the handful of greatest players in baseball history. They would surely have been chosen for the Hall on the first ballot if they had retired after the 1997 season.

But perhaps we place too much emphasis on consistency. In the early 1970s Frankie Frisch, himself a deserving Hall of Famer, used his position on the institution's Veterans Committee—essentially a back-door election process—to induct a number of his old teammates who had no valid claim for enshrinement. We can't "vote them off the island", but nor have we lowered the Hall's standards since then to elect every player better than, say, Freddie Lindstrom. We simply accept the mistakes, regret them, and move on. As Walt Whitman would re-

Larry Lambert/www.CartoonStock.com.

mind us, "Do I contradict myself? Very well then I contradict myself, (I am large, I contain multitudes.)"

Even if we were starting the Hall from scratch, though, the case against steroid users would be weak. It is true that Fay Vincent, a former commissioner of baseball, sent out a memorandum to teams in 1991 announcing that players would be prohibited from using any illegal drugs, including controlled substances used without a prescription. However, the missive was primarily aimed at recreational drugs—which were prevalent in the game in the 1980s—and Mr Vincent did not incorporate it into baseball's official rules, where the ban on doctoring baseballs can be found. Only in 2005 did the sport formally and specifically prohibit the use of a long list of substances, begin to test for them, and suspend players with positive results. Before then, using steroids in baseball was roughly analogous to, say, using Adderall for high-stress office work: you had to break the law to get it without a prescription, and it might harm your health in the long run, but no one would test you for it, or punish you if you got caught.

Given that system, staying clean would seem to be a greater offence for baseball players, who are paid to do everything within the rules to help their teams win, than taking steroids is. Bobby Abreu got raked over the coals for being reluctant to chase after deep fly balls for fear of crashing into the outfield wall. So why does, say, Lance Berkman, whom the press has lionised for his criticisms of steroid users, get a free pass for putting his team at a competitive disadvantage (assuming he in fact did not use PEDs)? At least Mr Abreu can claim he was trying to avoid an injury that would have harmed his club even more than failing to catch the ball would. In contrast, the likes of Mr Berkman prioritised their own well-being long after retirement over their teams' imperative to win now. Like all of us, professional athletes respond to incentives, and baseball players who doped did no more and no less than what they were paid to do.

The only way to prevent behaviour we disapprove of is to adjust the risk-return tradeoff so that it is no longer in people's interest to try. Fortunately, the lords of baseball belatedly stepped up to the plate and devised an admirably strict testing and punishment scheme. Just this January 10th the owners and players agreed to institute a new random testing programme for HGH. That certainly doesn't mean steroids have vanished from the game—just as suspensions for doctoring baseballs have not stopped pitchers of recent vintage from being suspected of applying foreign substances to the ball. But it does mean that players inclined to dope need to make sure they have the absolute finest pharmacists the dark side has to offer, and that one misstep could cost them far more than they could ever have hoped to gain by cheating. Just last year, Melky Cabrera was suspended for 50 games after testing positive for elevated levels of testosterone. Not only did he lose the chance to play for a team that wound up winning a championship, but he had to settle for a two-year, $16m contract this winter, a mere fraction of what he would have received had he not been caught.

Baseball is constantly evolving, and the Hall of Fame should honour the players who were most valuable in each era under the rules of the time. Ross Barnes was the premier position player of the 1870s thanks to his mastery of the "fair-foul bunt", a tactic that was eliminated by a rule change in 1877. Ed Walsh was arguably the best pitcher of the first decade of the 20th century because he reportedly could control the spitball so well he could hit a tack on a wall with it. In the 1920s and 30s Chuck Klein used to poke pitch after pitch over the right-field wall at Philadelphia's Baker Bowl, which was just 280 feet (85 metres) from home plate. And virtually all major league players until 1947 benefited from racial segregation. I'm just as curious to know how many home runs Babe Ruth would have hit if he had faced the likes of "Smokey" Joe Williams and "Bullet Joe" Rogan as I am to know how many homers Mr Bonds would have hit had he never used what he called "flaxseed oil".

Steroids may be unseemly, but they helped win games and championships for many years. Mr Bonds and his ilk should not be given a free pass for their chemical enhancements—the evidence that they took PEDs should be clearly stated on their Hall of Fame plaques. But there are few worse crimes for a museum than whitewashing history, which is what leaving them out entirely would amount to.

Periodical and Internet Sources Bibliography

The following articles have been selected to supplement the diverse views presented in this chapter.

Allen Barra	"Bonds, Clemens Must Be Forgiven," *Salon*, January 9, 2013.
Ian Crouch	"The Doomsday Ballot," *New Yorker*, November 28, 2012.
Aidan Ellis	"Would a Truth and Reconciliation Process Work for Cycling?," Law Brief Update, January 24, 2013.
Mike Hiserman	"Baseball Hall of Fame: Steroid Users Not Welcome Here," *Los Angeles Times*, January 9, 2013.
Tyler Kepner	"Steroid Era Suspicions Have Unfairly Tainted All," *New York Times*, January 6, 2013.
Jonah Keri	"The Fallacy of the Baseball Hall of Fame," Grantland, January 9, 2013.
Kevin Modesti	"Here's a Baseball Hall of Fame Vote for the 'Steroid Guys': Opinion," *Los Angeles Daily News*, January 8, 2013.
Ken Rosenthal	"Saying No to 'Roids in HOF, for Now," Fox Sports, December 30, 2012.
Chris Schad	"2013 Baseball Hall of Fame Vote: Why the Steroid Era Has Made Voters Gun-Shy," Bleacher Report, January 9, 2013.
Peter Schmuck	"Steroid Era Clouds Baseball Hall of Fame Voting," *Baltimore Sun*, December 22, 2013.
Dave Zirin	"The Baseball Hall of Fame's Epic Fail," *The Nation*, January 10, 2013.

For Further Discussion

Chapter 1

1. Do the risks of doping outweigh the benefits? In his viewpoint, Scott Douglas points out that there are real risks to doping. John Stossel argues that the risks of doping are exaggerated. Present your opinion after reading both viewpoints.

2. Many observers are concerned about the effect of doping on sport. Do you agree with Tim Burns that doping damages sports and athletic competition? Use information from his viewpoint to support your answer.

3. This chapter examines the reasons why athletes dope. Choose the main reason why you think athletes dope and explain your choice.

Chapter 2

1. Should doping be banned in sports? Provide a detailed answer, using information from the viewpoints in this chapter to support your opinion.

Chapter 3

1. Doping in sports has sparked a debate about athletes as role models. In his viewpoint, Kirk Mango contends that athletes who use performance-enhancing drugs should not be regarded as role models. In her viewpoint, Rochelle Ballin goes a step further, arguing that athletes should never be viewed as role models. What is your opinion about athletes as role models?

2. This chapter focuses on the effects of doping on sports. In your opinion which is the most damaging effect and why? Which one is the least damaging and why?

Chapter 4

1. In his viewpoint, Neil B. believes that there should be harsher punishments for athletes who dope. In her viewpoint, Kate Henne contends that prevention efforts and responsible regulation are preferable to punishment. Which approach do you think would be more effective and why?

2. After a series of devastating doping scandals, cycling has been struggling to move forward and get past its reputation as a dirty sport. In their viewpoint, Julian Savulescu and Bennett Foddy propose that a doping amnesty is necessary. In his viewpoint, John Leicester recommends the formation of a truth and reconciliation committee to address the problem. Do either one of these suggestions hold promise? Why or why not?

3. Should professional baseball players who used steroids during their career be eligible for induction into the National Baseball Hall of Fame and Museum? Explain your answer.

Organizations to Contact

The editors have compiled the following list of organizations concerned with the issues debated in this book. The descriptions are derived from materials provided by the organizations. All have publications or information available for interested readers. The list was compiled on the date of publication of the present volume; the information provided here may change. Be aware that many organizations take several weeks or longer to respond to inquiries, so allow as much time as possible.

International Association of Athletics Federations (IAAF)
14 rue Princesse Florestine, BP359, Monaco Cedex   MC 98007
+377 93 10 88 88 • fax: +377 93 15 95 15
website: www.iaaf.org

Founded in 1812, the International Association of Athletics Federations (IAAF) is the governing authority of the sport of track and field. It administers international track-and-field competitions, including the World Championships, the World Junior Championships, the Continental Cup, and the Hammer Throw Challenge. The IAAF is a leader in the antidoping movement, developing and applying a sophisticated antidoping program involving the testing of athletes in and out of competition. It also works closely with the World Anti-Doping Agency, the International Olympic Committee, and national sports federations to maximize antidoping efforts in track-and-field sports. The IAAF website offers details about its antidoping campaign, including information on testing protocol, prohibited substances, and educational materials.

International Cycling Union (UCI)
Ch. de la Melee 12, Aigle   1860
   Switzerland
+41 24 468 58 11 • fax: +41 24 468 58 12
e-mail: admin@uci.ch
website: www.uci.ch

Founded in 1900, the International Cycling Union (UCI) is cycling's international federation, responsible for promoting and administering the sport of cycling in cooperation with national federations. The ICU website provides the World Anti-Doping Agency's rules on doping, including a prohibited substances list, and offers information on testing procedures and policies. The site also features videos, an events calendar, statistics on recent races, and updates on training and development.

International Federation of Pharmaceutical Manufacturers & Associations (IFPMA)
15, Chemin Louis-Dunant, PO Box 195, Geneva 20 1211
  Switzerland
+41 22 338 3200 • fax: +41 22 338 3299
e-mail: info@ifpma.org
website: www.ifpma.org

The International Federation of Pharmaceutical Manufacturers & Associations (IFPMA) is a nonprofit, nongovernmental organization that represents the global, research-based pharmaceutical industry. The IFPMA's mission is to advocate for "policies that encourage discovery of and access to life-saving and life-enhancing medicines to improve the health of people everywhere." To that end, it promotes industry standards for manufacturing and quality assurance, encourages innovation, and fosters collaborative relationships and partnerships with international organizations. The IFPMA works with the World Anti-Doping Agency to discourage doping in sports by sharing information about new performance-enhancing drugs, monitoring their development, and ensuring their safe use. The IFPMA website offers information on a range of programs, policies, and campaigns; it also provides access to recent publications, a blog, and a calendar of upcoming events.

International Olympic Committee (IOC)

Chateau de Vidy, Case Postale 356, Lausanne   1001
  Switzerland
+41 21 621 6111 • fax: +41 21 621 6116
website: www.olympics.com/ioc

The International Olympic Committee (IOC) organizes and runs the Olympic Games, working with the athletes, the National Olympic Committees, the International Sports Federations, the United Nations, broadcasting partners, and the Organizing Committees for the Olympic Games. Globally it supports programs and competitions that favor diversity, encourages the participation of women in sport, teaches sporting ethics and fair play, and protects the rights and health of athletes. The IOC and its partners are on the front line of the fight against doping in sport, developing sophisticated testing procedures and updating methods and procedures to detect cheating athletes. The IOC website provides a wealth of information on past and upcoming Olympic Games, Olympic sports, Olympic athletes, and the Olympic legacy.

Major League Baseball (MLB)

245 Park Avenue, Thirty-First Floor, New York, NY   10167
(212) 931-7800 • fax: (212) 949-5654
website: http://mlb.mlb.com

Major League Baseball (MLB) is the professional baseball league for professional baseball players; it is made up of thirty teams that are split between two leagues. MLB coordinates and determines the schedule of regular and play-off games; organizes the annual All Star game and associated activities; hires umpires and other support staff; works with broadcast networks, radio, and other media outlets to broadcast games; markets teams, leagues, and players; negotiates policies and enforces regulations on steroids; and works with team owners on a wide range of issues to maintain a financially successful professional baseball league in the United States and Canada. The MLB website offers information on the league's philanthropic initiatives, press releases, and the rules of baseball.

National Basketball Association (NBA)
645 Fifth Avenue, New York, NY 10022
(212) 407-8000
website: www.nba.com

The National Basketball Association (NBA) is the professional basketball league in the United States and Canada. The NBA coordinates the regular season and postseason game schedules for the thirty teams that make up the league; organizes the annual All Star game and associated activities; negotiates contracts with broadcast networks, radio, and other media outlets to broadcast games; licenses and merchandises NBA products; markets the teams, leagues, and players; enforces league rules; hires and manages league officials; and works with team owners on a wide range of issues to maintain a financially successful professional basketball league. The NBA website provides the league's schedule, statistics, player blogs, videos, mobile apps, and photos.

National Collegiate Athletics Association (NCAA)
700 West Washington Street, PO Box 6222
Indianapolis, IN 46206
(317) 917-6222 • fax: (317) 917-6888
website: www.ncaa.org

The National Collegiate Athletics Association (NCAA) is a membership organization of colleges and universities that supports student athletes in the United States and Canada. The NCAA administers an extensive antidoping program, including drug testing. Its website provides a prohibited substances list, drug testing results, and information on the drug-testing appeals process.

National Football League (NFL)
345 Park Avenue, New York, NY 10017
(212) 450-2000
website: www.nfl.com

The National Football League (NFL) is the professional league for football in the United States. The league consists of thirty-two teams split between the American Football Conference and the National Football Conference. The NFL schedules and coordinates preseason, regular season, and playoff game games; formulates, monitors, and enforces rules; negotiates contracts with television, radio, and other media outlets for broadcast of NFL games; licenses and merchandises products; and works closely with team owners on a wide range of issues to maintain a safe, profitable, and exciting level of competition. The NFL website is packed with information on players, teams, and league history. It also offers podcasts, videos, blogs, and fan forums.

National Hockey League (NHL)
1185 Sixth Avenue, New York, NY   10036
(212) 789-2000
website: www.nhl.com

Founded in 1917, the National Hockey League (NHL) is the top league for professional ice hockey in the United States and Canada. The NHL operates a league of thirty hockey clubs with players from more than twenty countries around the world. The NHL schedules and manages preseason, regular season, and play-off games; makes and enforces rules; sets policy; negotiates contracts with television, radio, and other media outlets for broadcast of NHL games; licenses and merchandises products; and works closely with team owners on a wide range of issues to maintain a safe, profitable, and exciting level of competition on the ice. The NHL website offers rosters, statistics, schedules, live game radio broadcasts, and video clips.

Office of National Drug Control Policy (ONDCP)
c/o The White House, 1600 Pennsylvania Avenue, NW
Washington, DC   20500
(202) 456-1111
website: www.whitehouse.gov/ondcp

The Office of National Drug Control Policy (ONDCP) develops and coordinates public-health strategies to fight drug abuse and address the economic, political, social, and health consequences of drug addiction. It also publishes *National Drug Control Strategy*, an annual report on the nation's approach to drug policy. The ONDCP website features a blog that provides updates on initiatives and drug policy.

United States Anti-Doping Agency (USADA)
5555 Tech Center Drive, Suite 200
Colorado Springs, CO   80919
(866) 601-2632 • fax: (719) 785-2001
e-mail: usada@usada.org
website: www.usada.org

The United States Anti-Doping Agency (USADA) is a nongovernmental, national antidoping agency for Olympic and Paralympic sports. It administers drug tests to athletes participating in the Olympic and Paralympics. The USADA website offers information on how to educate athletes on their antidoping responsibilities, including information on prohibited substances, testing methods, and dietary guidelines. It also offers the biannual e-newsletter, *Spirit of Sport*.

USA Track & Field (USATF)
132 East Washington Street, Suite 800
Indianapolis, TN   46204
(317) 261-0500 • fax: (317) 261-0481
website: www.usatf.org

The USA Track & Field (USATF) is the governing body for track and field, long-distance running, and race walking in the United States. The USATF chooses American athletes to compete in international competitions, including the Olympics; develops young athletes through the junior Olympic programs; establishes and enforces rules and regulations regarding the sport; certifies race venues and courses; validates athletic records; and sanctions more that four thousand local, regional, state, and national events every year. The USATF coordinates a proactive antidoping program with the World Anti-Doping Agency, the United States Anti-Doping Agency, the International Olympic Committee, the International Association of Athletics Federations, and other international and national agencies. The USATF website offers information on its antidoping program, including educational materials, drug-testing procedures and standards, and prohibited substances.

World Anti-Doping Agency (WADA)
800 Place Victoria, Suite 1700, PO Box 120
Montreal   H4Z 1B7
   Canada
(514) 904-9232 • fax: (514) 904-8650
website: www.wada-ama.org

Founded in 1999, the World Anti-Doping Agency (WADA) is an independent, international agency that promotes, coordinates, and monitors the fight against doping in sports. WADA formulated the World Anti-Doping Code, a standard set of rules that regulate antidoping efforts by international sports federations, national sports federations and antidoping organizations, the International Olympic Committee, and the International Paralympic Committee. The code has been adopted by more than six hundred federations and committees around the world. The WADA pursues a comprehensive approach to fighting doping in sports, and information about a range of antidoping activities is available on the agency's website. Also available is WADA's list of prohibited substances, guidelines on drug testing, rules and regulations about doping and other medical issues, a digital library, and educational materials. The WADA's flagship magazine, *Play True* is also available on the website.

Bibliography of Books

Reed Albergotti

Wheelman: Lance Armstrong, the Tour de France, and the Greatest Sports Conspiracy Ever. New York: Gotham, 2013.

Rob Beamish

Steroids: A New Look at Performance-Enhancing Drugs. Santa Barbara, CA: Praeger, 2011.

Graham Brooks, Azeem Aleem, and Mark Button

Fraud, Corruption and Sport. New York: Palgrave Macmillan, 2013.

Dwain Chambers

Race Against Me: My Story. Luton, England: Andrews UK, 2010.

Chris E. Cooper

Run, Swim, Throw, Cheat: The Science Behind Drugs in Sport. Oxford: Oxford University Press, 2013.

Paul David

A Guide to the World Anti-Doping Code: The Fight for the Spirit of Sport, 2nd ed. Cambridge: Cambridge University Press, 2013.

Michael Dennis and Jonathan Grix

Sport Under Communism: Behind the East German "Miracle". New York: Palgrave Macmillan, 2013.

David J. Epstein

The Sports Gene: Inside the Science of Extraordinary Athletic Performance. New York: Current, 2013.

Jim Gullo

Trading Manny: How a Father and Son Learned to Love Baseball Again. Boston: De Capo Press, 2012.

Tyler Hamilton
and Daniel Coyle

The Secret Race: Inside the Hidden World of the Tour de France. New York: Bantam Books, 2012.

Thomas M. Hunt
and John M.
Hoberman

Drug Games: The International Olympic Committee and the Politics of Doping, 1960–2008. Austin: University of Texas Press, 2011.

Juliet Macur

Cycle of Lies: The Definitive Inside Story of the Fall of Lance Armstrong. London: HarperCollins, 2013.

Jason Mazanov

Toward a Social Science of Drugs in Sport. London: Routledge, 2012.

David Millar

Racing Through the Dark. New York: Touchstone, 2012.

Vernor Moller

The Ethics of Doping and Anti-Doping: Redeeming the Soul of Sport. New York: Routledge, 2010.

Gerry Moore

The Little Black Bottle: Choppy Warburton, the Question of Doping, and the Death of His Bicycle Racers. San Francisco: Van der Plas, 2011.

Richard Moore

The Dirtiest Race in History: Ben Johnson, Carl Lewis, and the 1988 Olympic 100m Final. London: Wisden, 2013.

Daniel M. Rosen

Dope: A History of Performance Enhancement in Sports from the Nineteenth Century to Today. Westport, CT: Praeger, 2008.

Bob Steward and Aaron Smith — *Rethinking Drug Use in Sport: Why the War Will Never Be Won*. New York: Routledge, 2014.

Bill Strickland — *Tour de Lance: The Extraordinary Story of Lance Armstrong's Fight to Reclaim the Tour de France*. New York: Harmony Books, 2010.

Andrew Tilin — *The Doper Next Door: My Strange and Scandalous Year on Performance-Enhancing Drugs*. Berkeley: Counterpoint, 2011.

David Walsh — *Seven Deadly Sins: My Pursuit of Lance Armstrong*. New York: Atria Books, 2012.

Index